CHEAP
SLEEPS
in PARIS

SANDRA A. GUSTAFSON

CHRONICLE BOOKS

SAN FRANCISCO

Printed in the United States of America

Library of Congress Cataloging-in-Publication Data available.

ISBN 0-8118-0058-X

Editing: Carolyn Miller
Cover design: Robin Weiss
Cover photograph: © Francisco Hidalgo/ The Image Bank
Cover map: Historic Urban Plans, Ithaca, NY
Book design: Words & Deeds

Distributed in Canada by
Raincoast Books
112 East Third Avenue
Vancouver, B.C. V5T 1C8

10 9 8 7 6 5 4 3 2

Chronicle Books
275 Fifth Street
San Francisco, CA 94103

For Pete

CONTENTS

TO THE READER

There is never any ending to Paris. Each person who is touched by the charm of this enchanting city carries away special memories and a lifetime of pleasant dreams.

— Ernest Hemingway, *A Moveable Feast*

Whether seen for the first or the fifteenth time, Paris is a never-ending love affair. Many Americans savor returning to the Paris they treasure, to renew longstanding passions or to develop new ones. Walk a block, turn a corner—in Paris there is always something interesting, something beautiful and new, or something that has been there forever, but which you never noticed until now. No matter what time of year you visit, it is impossible to keep from falling in love with the city, its grand boulevards, the beautiful women, the breathtaking monuments, the glorious food, the fabulous art, and the sweeping view from Place de la Concorde up the Champs-Élysées or from the steps of Sacré-Coeur over the entire city. The American passion for France has now entered its third century; it continues through wars, riots, occupations, and the rise and fall of hemlines and the dollar. La Belle France beckons us, no matter what.

Whatever type of accommodation you are looking for, you will find it in Paris. The city has more than 1,700 hotels, with a total of 11,700 rooms in the one-star to four-star range. This excludes no-star hotels, pensions, bed and breakfasts in private homes, student lodgings, residence hotels, and apartment rentals for tourists. The essence of any Parisian hotel is its individuality, and no two are exactly alike. They vary from the most luxurious pleasure palaces in the world to some few people would consider. It is possible, of course, to check into the Hilton or any other big-name chain hotel, but only in Paris can you stay along the Seine in a quaint 17th-century hotel with picture-postcard views of Notre-Dame, or at the famed Ritz on Place Vendôme, where there are more than four employees for every guest and rates that deliberately exceed the means of most mortals.

It is true that a trip to Paris will cost more today than it did several years ago, but what doesn't? Europe—or Paris—on $5 or $10 a day no longer exists for any traveler. Most of those romantically threadbare hotels of our youth are gone for good. Yet there are still many ways to save money and maximize the buying strength of the dollar without feeling *nouveau pauvre* in the process.

Cheap Sleeps in Paris is not a list of the cheapest beds in Paris. Those have been covered in other guidebooks directed toward travelers for whom price is more important than comfort, cleanliness, or convenience. The purpose of this book is to offer fail-safe advice, for the first-time visitor and the Paris veteran, on finding hotels that are in keeping with a variety of daily needs, tastes, and budgets. In the listings, there are hotels for lovers and honeymooners, nostalgia buffs, backpackers, and families, from the center of Paris to the fringes. Other options include camping in the Bois de Boulogne, renting an apartment, staying in a private home, or living in a student dormitory. Each selection was included because I felt it had something special to offer. Some represent a particular style or era; others have been beautifully restored. Some are in non-tourist neighborhoods where people live and work, send their children to school, get their cars repaired, and go to the dentist. Some can be termed basic, many are charming, and a few are starkly modern. Many are cheap, others not so cheap, and a few fall into the Big Splurge category for those with more flexible budgets and demanding tastes. All have one vital feature in common: the potential for providing a memorable stay that will make you feel you have discovered your own part of the real Paris.

It is important for readers to know that no hotel can purchase a listing or ask to be included in this book, and that I do all the research for *Cheap Sleeps* myself. On my last trip to Paris, I personally inspected every hotel in this current edition, along with hundreds of others that did not make the final cut for one reason or another. What are the guidelines that I use for selecting a hotel? The primary concern is value for money, followed by cleanliness, location, and management attitude. During my research, I walked hundreds of miles and talked with countless hotel owners, managers, receptionists, maids, guests, and leaders in the travel and tourist industry in Paris. On my visits to the hotels, which were always unannounced, I wiped my fingers across the door tops, inspected closets, turned on the showers, checked for thin towels and waxed or sandy toilet paper, opened and closed windows, bounced on beds and looked under them for dust, stumbled along dimly lit corridors and climbed seemingly endless flights of stairs. The result is this latest edition of *Cheap Sleeps in Paris,* which will show you how to cut corners in style, so that traveling on a budget won't mean giving up the good life or lowering your standards.

In addition to giving the value-conscious traveler the inside track to some of the best hotel values in Paris, *Cheap Sleeps in Paris* offers insider information on shopping. If you, like me, believe the eighth deadly sin is paying full retail price for anything, then you will love the "Cheap Chic" shopping section in the back of the book. Here you will find everything from designer discount shops and big-name cosmetics to the latest models of shoes, all at a fraction of their regular cost, as well as information on where to rent a formal ball gown for an evening on the town.

The goal of *Cheap Sleeps in Paris* is to give enough background information to help you select the right hotel to make your stay in Paris truly special, thus setting the stage for many return visits. If I have been able to do that, I will have done my job well. I wish you *bonne chance* and *bon voyage!*

General Information

TIPS FOR CHEAP SLEEPS IN PARIS

1. For two weeks in mid-January and mid-February, May, June, September, and October are the hardest months to find a hotel room in Paris. Try to go during the off season, when rates and air fares are at their lowest.

2. Unless you enjoy standing in long lines in French government tourist offices, or wandering the streets looking for a hotel, never even consider arriving in Paris without confirmed hotel reservations *in writing.*

3. Back rooms often face grim walls or dreary courtyards and are often smaller, but they cost less and are quieter.

4. Always check out the room before you check in. Confirm the rate and discuss the cost of any extras ahead of time, not when paying the bill. Know that all hotels must clearly post their rates by the reception desk.

5. Twin beds cost more than a double, and any room with a private shower will be less than one with a bathtub.

6. Avoid eating breakfast at your hotel. Instead, join the Parisians standing at the zinc bar at the corner café. Be sure to inform the hotel at the beginning of your stay that you will not be eating breakfast, and see to it that the cost is deducted (per person, per day) from your entire bill. Only a few hotels will refuse to deduct breakfast, but you must ask: it is never done voluntarily.

7. Don't drink the beverages from the mini-bar. Remove them and put in your own, purchased from the corner grocery store.

8. Do your own laundry and take your cleaning to the neighborhood dry cleaner yourself. Laundry and dry cleaning sent from the hotel can be wildly expensive and blow a budget to shreds.

9. Notify the hotel if you expect to arrive after 6 P.M. Even if you have paid the room deposit, the hotel can technically give your room away to someone else if they haven't heard from you as to your arrival time.

10. Change money at a bank, *never* at a hotel.

11. Avoid at all costs going through the hotel switchboard when calling home. Surcharges can add up to 100 percent of the cost of the call. Instead, use USA DIRECT: Dial 19, wait for the dial tone, and then dial 0011. An English-speaking AT&T operator will answer. Tell her if you want the call to be collect, or you can pay for it using a domestic AT&T calling card number. This is simple, painless, and definitely the least expensive way to go.

12. An extra bed cannot cost more than 30 percent of the room price.

13. Ask what the refund policy is if you have sent a deposit and have to cancel at the last minute or before. Some of the smaller hotels have draconian ideas about refunds.

HIGH AND LOW SEASONS

How wonderful it would be to be able to drop everything and fly to Paris whenever the spirit moved us! If such romantic impulses don't quite fit into your schedule or budget, then the high and low seasons must be taken into consideration. These particular times of the year affect not only the availability of hotel rooms and rates, but airline fares as well. The best time is the off season in early spring or late autumn, when most of the other tourists have gone home and everything is easier to come by, including Métro seats, café tables, and good-natured waiters.

For about two weeks in mid-January and mid-February, fashion showings fill the city to the bursting point, and many hotels charge higher rates. Dates vary slightly from year to year, so the best bet is to check with the French Government Tourist Office in New York or Los Angeles for the latest information. During July and August, you will be sharing your Parisian holiday with many other tourists and very few French. Despite government pleadings and tourist demands, August is still the traditional vacation month for Parisians, and many restaurants and shops are closed.

FRENCH HOLIDAYS

Holidays (*les jours fériés*) are vital dates to bear in mind when planning any trip to Paris. First, the banks are usually closed a half day before each holiday, as well as the day after in some instances. Second, the traffic is horrendous, especially if the holiday falls on a Tuesday or Thursday, when many French will take Monday or Friday off as well. Most shops, many restaurants, and some museums are closed. Skeleton or third-string crews man the hotel desks, and there is often a laid-back attitude during a holiday period, resulting in quick excuses for places being closed and things not working. It can all add up to some very frustrating times for a traveler.

New Year's Day (January 1)	*Jour de l'An*
Easter Sunday and Monday	*Pâques* and *Lundi de Pâques*
Labor Day (May 1)	*Fête du Travail*
VE Day (May 8)	*Armistice* 1945
Ascension Day (40 days after Easter)	*Ascension*
Pentecost (seventh Sunday after Easter) and Pentecost Monday	*Pentecôte* and *Lundi de Pentecôte*
Bastille Day (July 14)	*Quatorze Juillet/Fête Nationale*
Assumption Day (August 15)	*Assomption*
All Saints' Day (November 1)	*Toussaint*
Armistice Day (November 11)	*Armistice* 1918
Christmas Day (December 25)	*Noël*

For motorists, the time to avoid is the last weekend in August, when the *grand rentrée* of Parisian vacationers creates traffic snarls of world-class proportions.

RESERVATIONS

People often ask, "Do I need advance hotel reservations in Paris?" The answer is yes, positively! In order to be assured of a room, you *must* reserve as far in advance as possible. Paris can be one of the worst hotel bottlenecks in Europe, and a confirmed reservation, even on the slowest day in the low season, will save you frantic hours spent searching for a room after arrival. It will also save you money, because without advance reservations you will probably be forced to take something beyond your budget, perhaps in a part of the city that you don't like.

The easiest way to reserve is to let your travel agent do all the work. However, it is not hard to do it yourself, and frankly it is better, because you will be able to ask questions, inquire about exact rates, and arrange just what you want before leaving the comfort of your own home. Today, the best way to reserve is by fax, telex, or telephone, followed by a guarantee with a major credit card, an international money order, or, in a few cases, a money order in French francs.

No matter how you decide to make your reservation, the following points should be covered in your inquiry:

1. Dates of stay, time of arrival, and number of persons in the party.

2. Size and type of room (double or twin beds, extra beds, adjoining rooms, suite, etc.).

3. Facilities needed: private toilet, shower and/or bathtub, or hall facilities if acceptable.

4. Location of room: view, on the street, on the courtyard, or in the back of the hotel.

5. Rates. Determine what the nightly rate will be and state whether you will be eating breakfast at the hotel (remember, you will save money if you don't).

6. Deposit required and form of payment.

7. Request a confirmation in writing from the hotel for your reservation, and for your deposit, if required, and carry it with you to the registration desk. This avoids a multitude of possible problems on arrival.

FAX

If you have access to a fax machine, and the hotel has a fax number (sometimes called a *télécopie* number), this is the latest and certainly one of the best ways to secure a confirmed booking. To fax a message to Paris, dial 011-33-1 and then the fax number of the hotel.

TELEX

If you or your travel agent would prefer sending a telex and the hotel has one, this is a cheap and reliable way to reserve because it gives you a complete record of your exchanges with the hotel. Be sure to take the hotel's telex response with you to Paris; it is your letter of confirmation.

TELEPHONE

Always make the call during the hotel's weekday business hours to avoid talking to a night clerk who has no authority to make reservations from abroad. Before calling, write down all your requests and questions. Ask the hotel to send you a written confirmation, and, in turn, send them a letter confirming your telephone reservation. Send the letter certified, so you will know they received it, and keep a copy. In your letter to the hotel, cite the details of the conversation, the name of the person with whom you spoke, and the date and time of the call, and enclose a deposit if they do not accept a credit card number as a room guarantee. To dial direct to Paris from an AT&T phone, dial 011-33-1, followed by the number given in the listing for the hotel. If you are dialing from another telephone system (i.e., Sprint, etc.), dial 1-0-288-011-33-1 and the number of the hotel.

LETTER

Transatlantic mail can take more than two weeks each way. If there is a strike along the way, who knows how long mail will take to reach its destination. When you consider the entire cost of the trip against the cost of a fax, telex, or telephone call, it amounts to a very small percentage. In today's electronic world, writing for reservations seems as old-fashioned as wearing a bustle. If you do decide to reserve by mail, allow sufficient time for a response and for making alternate plans if necessary. The following letter should cover all the bases.

Dear Sir:

I would like to reserve __ room(s) (that is quiet) (on the garden/the street/ the courtyard) with two beds (with one big bed/one regular-sized bed) with bath and toilet (with shower and toilet, without shower and toilet) for __night(s) beginning on __ to __. I would like to have the room(s) include (without) breakfast. You will find attached __F as a deposit (my credit card number as a deposit___).

Would you please be kind enough to confirm this reservation as soon as possible? Thank you for your assistance.

Yours sincerely,

Monsieur:

Je voudrais réserver __ chambre(s) (tranquille) qui donne sur le jardin/la rue/ la cour) à deux lits (avec un grand lit/à un lit) avec salle de bains et WC (avec douche et WC/sans douche et WC) pour ___ nuit(s) à partir du __ au__. Je voudrais prendre la chambre(s) avec (sans) le petit déjeuner. Vous trouvez ci-joint ___F à titre d'arrhes.

Auriez-vous le bonté de bien vouloir me confirmer cette réservation dès que possible? Je vous remercie de votre obligeance, et je vous prie de croire, Monsieur, à l'assurance de mes sentiments distingués.

DEPOSITS

After accepting your reservation, most hotels will require at least a one-night deposit, even if you have been a guest there before. This is smart insurance for both sides. The easiest way to handle a deposit is with a credit card. If the hotel does not take credit cards, there are other options. The next best thing is sending the hotel an American Express international money order in U.S. dollars. This can be converted into French francs by the hotel and saves you having to secure a deposit in French francs from this side of the Atlantic. While this option is more convenient for the traveler, it is added work for the hotel, and some, especially in the lower price ranges, simply refuse. If your hotel insists on a deposit in French francs only, you will have to deal with that through your local bank.

LATE ARRIVALS

Hotel guests are expected to arrive by 6 P.M. If you have a reservation, even with a deposit, the hotel does not always hold the room for you beyond this time. To allow for travel delays, state when making reservations that you may arrive after 6 P.M., and ask the hotel to hold your room. If arriving by plane or train, give the hotel the airline and flight number or the train arrival time and the train station (there are five in Paris). Asking for the room to be held will usually oblige you to pay for it, even if you don't arrive until the next morning.

MONEY MATTERS

If you remember to carry traveler's checks, charge big items on your credit card, convert to francs as you go, and use ATMs for incidental cash, you will do fine. Also, remember to carry a few of your own personal checks. If you suddenly run out of money, you can use them to get cash advances, provided the credit card you have allows this. Try to have a few francs on hand when you arrive. This gets you out of the airport faster and keeps you from having to wait in line to get enough francs to get into Paris. True, you may pay more for this convenience, but if you change only $100 or so before you leave home, you will never miss the few cents extra this may cost.

CURRENCY EXCHANGE

Estimate your needs carefully. If you overbuy in francs, you will lose twice, buying and then selling. Every time you change money, someone is making a profit, and, I assure you, it isn't you. Your best currency exchange rate will be at a bank. You will always get a better rate from traveler's checks than for cash, but the real cost lies in what you spent to get the traveler's checks in the first place. If your bank gives free American Express traveler's checks, you can cash them commission free at the American Express office in Paris. The only drawback here is that the lines are slow and oh so long! The office is at 11, rue Scribe (9th), Métro Opéra; open Monday through Friday from 9 A.M. to 5 P.M. and Saturday from 9 A.M. to noon. The worst rates are at the airport. The second-worst rates are at hotels, restaurants, and shops. Banking hours are Monday through Friday, 9:30 A.M. to 4:30 P.M. Many banks close at noon the day before a public holiday and remain closed the day after Christmas and Easter. The following banks are open longer hours and give competitive rates.

Banque Niçoise de Credit	8, boulevard de la Madeleine (8th); Métro Madeleine; Mon–Sat 9 A.M.–6 P.M.; no commission charged
TWA Office, Champs-Élysées	Champs-Élysées (8th); Métro George V; Mon–Sat 9 A.M.–6 P.M.; no commission charged
CCF	115, avenue Champs-Élysées (8th); Métro George V; Mon–Sat 9 A.M.–8 P.M.

| Société Financière de Change | 11, rue Lincoln (8th); Métro George V; Mon–Fri 10 A.M.–midnight, Sat and Sun 10 A.M.–8:30 P.M. |

If you need money in the middle of a Sunday night or at some other odd hour, go to the 24-hour-a-day, 7-days-a-week currency exchange at:

| Bred Bank | Galerie Pont Show, Change Automatique; 66, avenue des Champs-Élysées (8th); Métro Franklin D. Roosevelt. Put in your dollars and out will come French francs. Only U.S. $10 or $20 bills are accepted, so this should be used only for emergencies. |

You can also change money at various authorized money-changers' offices, which are thick in the tourist areas. They often advertise "commission-free" exchanges, but the rates are low. Best bet with these is to shop around to find the highest rate.

CREDIT CARDS

For the most part, I recommend using a credit card whenever possible. The benefits are many. It is the safest way because it eliminates the need for carrying large sums of cash that must be purchased by standing in a long line at a bank or another money-changing facility. It also provides you with a record of your purchases, and, best of all, you often get delayed billing of up to four to six weeks after the purchase. If you pay in cash, the money is gone immediately. With a credit card, the money stays in your bank account, drawing interest until you need it to pay the final bill. The credit card company gives the best rate of exchange on the day the receipt from the purchase is submitted, and this can also work to your advantage if the dollar is rising. Every *Cheap Sleeps in Paris* listing states whether or not plastic money is accepted in that hotel or Cheap Chic shop. Thankfully, most two- and three-star hotels accept one major credit card. If, heaven forbid, you happen to lose a credit card, call one of these 24-hour hotlines in Paris to report the loss:

American Express	47-08-31-21, 47-77-72-00
Diners Club	47-62-75-75
MasterCard (Eurocard)	43-23-47-47

Visa (Carte Bleu)	42-77-11-90
Outside Paris	(16) 54-42-12-12

Emergency personal check cashing is a benefit for many card holders, as are free travel insurance and car rental insurance. Check with your issuing bank to determine the benefits you have—you may be pleasantly surprised.

TIPPING

How much is too much, and what is enough? Here are a few guidelines.

In France, a service charge of 12 to 15 percent is added to hotel and restaurant bills. While this eliminates the need for tips in general, there are certain times when a tip is appropriate.

Bar, cafés, restaurants	You may leave a few extra francs if the service has been exceptional.
Hotels	Bellboy, 5F per bag; maid about 20F for a three-day stay; room service 10F.
Hairdressers	10–15 percent.
Taxi drivers	10–15 percent.
Theater usher	2–3F for seating 2 people.

Note: Beware of the Tipping Scam. There is an increasingly common practice (especially in restaurants) of putting the entire amount of the bill to which a 12 to 15 percent service has *already* been added in the top box of the charge slip, leaving the boxes marked tip and total empty. Don't be intimidated. Draw a line from the top figure to the total and then write in the total yourself. If you are leaving a tip on top of the total, leave it in cash. Often tips left on credit cards are not properly distributed.

The bottom line on tipping in Paris is the same as in any place else in the world: It is a matter of personal choice. If you liked the service, reward it; if not, don't feel guilty about not leaving a single *sou*.

TRANSPORTATION

GETTING INTO PARIS FROM THE AIRPORTS

Roissy-Charles de Gaulle Airport: 47-58-20-18 (transportation information), 48-62-12-12 (flight information).

Air France operates out of Terminal 1 and all the other airlines from Terminal 2.

A taxi is the easiest and most comfortable and expensive way to go. It takes about 50 minutes, but during rush hours, add at least 30 more minutes and more francs to play it safe. Fares range from 150 to 200F during the day; from 8 P.M. to 7 A.M., the tab will double.

A more economical way is by the direct RER train, which leaves every 15 minutes for Gare du Nord (10th), Chatelet (1st), Luxembourg (5th), Port-Royal (5th), and Denfert-Rochereau (14th). A typical fare is around 40F.

There is also the Air France shuttle bus, which drops passengers near the Arc de Triomphe for about 40F. The problem with this is that you then have to hail a cab, and it is not a very easy location for doing so.

Going back to Roissy-Charles de Gaulle, Air France buses leave every 15 minutes from the bus terminal in the basement of the Palais des Congrès at Porte-Maillot. Allow 1 hour for the trip.

Orly Airport: 45-50-32-30 (transportation information), 48-67-12-34 (flight information).

Orly has two terminals: *Sud* (South) for international flights and *Ouest* (West) for domestic flights.

Air France buses leave Orly Sud every 12 minutes from Exit 1 and go to the Invalides terminal in Paris. From here you can easily get on the Métro or take a taxi to your hotel. The cost of the bus is around 30F.

Another shuttle bus leaves Orly every 15 minutes and drops passengers at the Orly RER terminal. There you get on the RER train for a 30-minute trip to the Invalides terminal. This costs 35F.

A taxi from Orly into Paris costs about 150F during the day and more at night.

To return to Orly, there is an Air France bus leaving every 15 minutes from the Invalides terminal. The trip takes 30 minutes if there is no traffic, but you should allow at least an hour during rush hour.

MÉTRO

The Paris Métro system is one of the best in the world. It can take you within walking distance of almost everywhere you want to go in the city. Trains run from 5:30 A.M. to 12:15 A.M. You can buy individual tickets, but a *carnet* of ten is much more practical. If you are staying in Paris for more than a few days, get the weekly *Coupon Jaune* or the monthly *Carte Orange*. Both allow unlimited travel on the Métro and buses. To get either one you must have a photo (there are photo booths in some Métro stations, but it is better to bring a few from home). You may buy all of your tickets for the Métro or the bus at the ticket counter in any Métro station or from the Bureau de Tourisme RATP, place de la Madeleine (8th), Métro Madeleine (open Monday through Saturday 7:30 A.M. to 7 P.M., Sunday and holidays 6:30 A.M. to 6 P.M.). This office also has bus and Métro maps. For the most detailed bus and Métro routes, consult the *Plan de Paris par Arrondissement* (see page 29).

BUS

Because the Métro is so fast and efficient, visitors often overlook the buses. Buses use the same tickets as the Métro. All buses run from 7:30 A.M. to 8:30 P.M. The Noctambus runs all night, but the routes are fewer. The pamphlet printed by the RATP—*Paris Bus, Métro, RER Routes*—lists several scenic bus routes and directions to major museums, churches, and monuments.

TAXIS

If the light on the taxi roof is on, the taxi is available. Often the challenge of finding a taxi in Paris rivals that in New York City on a busy Friday afternoon. The chances of hailing a taxi on the street corner are slim to none—better go to a taxi stand or call:

Taxi Bleu	46-36-10-10
Taxi Étoile	42-70-41-41
Taxi for handicapped (24 hours)	48-37-85-85

If you want an early-morning taxi to take you to the airport, book it the night before.

If you do call a taxi, the fare starts when the driver gets the call, not when you get in.

WHAT TO WEAR

Naturally you will leave your heavy wool coat and long johns at home when you visit Paris in August. But what kind of light coat makes sense in May or June? USA *Today* has a weather hotline (900-300-USAT) that gives you the time, temperature, and weather forecasts as well as other travel information for 490 cities around the world.

If you follow only one piece of advice in *Cheap Sleeps in Paris*, let it be this: *travel light*. Porters are no longer roaming airports or train stations, and bellboys are also relics of the past for most hotels in the Cheap Sleep category. Therefore, *you* are going to have to carry your own luggage, and, believe me, less is definitely best. Take only half of what you think you will need, color coordinate it, and remember, this is Paris, not Mars, so you can run out and buy something wonderful if you need to fill in your travel wardrobe.

One of the favorite pastimes of Parisians and their expatriate friends is to sit in a café along a busy boulevard and pick out the tourists. You can spot them a mile away in summer in their tank tops and shorts, and in the winter bundled up in parkas as if the ski slopes were just around the next corner.

Parisians are some of the most stylish people on earth. They are also quite conservative in their dress. Yes, you will see some off-the-wall outfits on bionic bodies, but you will never see shorts on women or Bermudas on men in Paris. Big-city clothes are the call of the day, no matter what the weather may be. Men will feel comfortable wearing a jacket and slacks with a nice shirt or turtleneck. Ties are almost mandatory at the best restaurants. Women will feel best in simple well-tailored suits, dresses, skirts, or pant suits. Gauzy lime-green jumpsuits and jogging shoes spell *tourist*!

SENIOR-CITIZEN DISCOUNTS: CARTE VERMEIL

If you have reached your 60th birthday, in France you are a member of the *troisième age* (third age) and eligible for a Carte Vermeil (CV).

This card entitles you to a number of significant discounts, including reductions on air and rail travel as well as on the bus and Métro in Paris. The French domestic airline Air Inter honors "third agers" by giving up to 50 percent reductions on regular non-excursion ticket prices. On French trains, you can save between 24 percent and 50 percent of the cost of a first- or second-class compartment and 10 percent of an excursion ticket. These air and rail reductions are not available during all seasons of the year, but if you can get in on the savings, they can be significant. Other benefits include reduced entrance rates for theaters, museums, and cinemas. Wherever you go, ask if there are special rates for senior citizens; the answer will often be yes.

The Carte Vermeil is valid for one year from June 1 to May 31 of the following year. The cost is about $20. The card cannot be purchased in the United States but is available at any major railway station in France. Don't expect clerks to speak English, but you won't need much French to communicate your wishes, as Parisians are used to dealing with foreigners who are privy to this super deal. Be sure to take your passport as proof of age. For more information, contact French National Railroads, 610 Fifth Avenue, New York, NY 10020; telephone 212-582-2110.

PRACTICAL INFORMATION

EMERGENCY NUMBERS

The American Hospital	63, bd. Victor Hugo, Neuilly; Métro Pont de Neuilly; 47-47-53-00

The British Hospital	47-58-13-12
Search for hospitalized persons	40-27-30-81; 8:45 A.M.–5:30 P.M.
Burns	42-34-17-58 (24 hours)
Drug Crisis Center	05-05-88-88
Fire	Dial 18
Poison	42-05-63-29, 40-37-04-04 (24 hours)
Police	Dial 17
SAMU (Ambulance)	45-67-50-50
SOS Cardiac	45-45-41-00, 47-07-50-50
SOS Dentist	43-07-33-68, 43-37-51-00
SOS Doctor	43-37-77-77, 47-07-77-77
SOS Handicap (medical assistance for the handicapped)	47-41-37-57, 47-41-32-33, 47-41-20-74
SOS Lawyer	43-29-33-00; Mon–Fri 7–11 P.M.
SOS Nurse	48-87-77-77
SOS Eye	40-92-93-94
SOS Pediatric	Emergency pediatric doctors; will make house calls; 42-93-19-99; Mon–Fri 7 A.M.–midnight, Sat 2 P.M.–midnight, Sun and holidays 7 A.M.–midnight
SOS Tailor	40-15-03-14; Mon–Fri 9 A.M.–6 P.M.
24-hour pharmacy	Pharmacie Dhèry, 85, av. des Champs-Élysées (8th); Métro Franklin D. Roosevelt; open 365 days a year; 45-62-02-41
American Pharmacy	Pharmacie Anglo-Américaine, 6 rue Castiglione (1st); Métro Tuileries; open Mon–Sat 9 A.M.–7:30 P.M.

USEFUL NUMBERS

Alcoholics Anonymous	46-34-59-65
American Embassy	2, av. Gabriel (8th); Métro Concorde, 42-96-12-02
American Express	The pipeline to home, with bank, money exchange, tourist

	information and tours, and more: 11, rue Scribe (9th); Métro Opéra; open Mon–Fri 9 A.M.–5 P.M., Sat 9 A.M.–noon; 45-75-62-16
Complaints about a hotel	Direction du Tourisme, 2, rue Linois (15th); Métro Charles-Michels
Emergency car repair	42-57-33-44
Lost and Found	36, rue des Morillons (15th); Métro Convention; Mon–Fri 9 A.M.–6 P.M.; no information given over phone
Post Office (24 hours)	Hôtel des Postes, 52, rue du Louvre (1st); Métro Louvre; 40-28-20-00
Taxis	42-00-67-89, 42-02-42-02, 42-03-99-99
English-speaking telephone assistance:	
Long-distance operator	19-00-11
Crisis hotline	47-20-89-98, 47-23-80-80 (3–11 P.M. daily)
Time	44-63-84-00
Traffic	48-58-33-33
Weather	45-55-95-90
Underground version of 911: dial it and a sewer worker will try to rescue that key or diamond earring that fell through the manhole grate	44-66-49-25
Tourist information	Main office of French Government Tourist Office, 127, av. des Champs-Élysées (8th); Métro Charles de Gaulle-Étoile; summer hours 9 A.M.–9 P.M. daily; winter hours 9 A.M.–6 P.M. daily; 47-23-61-72
French Government Tourist Offices in the U.S.	610 Fifth Ave., New York, NY 10020; 212-757-1125 9454 Wilshire Blvd., Beverly Hills, CA 90212; 213-271-6665

A FEW LAST-MINUTE HINTS

1. In France, the ground floor (*rez-de-chaussée*) is what Americans call the first floor; the French first floor (*premier étage*) is our second floor.

2. Let's face it, sometimes things are lost or stolen. If you lose your passport, you not only must replace it immediately, you must also show proof of citizenship. This is not easy to do when all of your documents citing proof are gone. To be prepared for such calamities, I always take a xeroxed copy of my passport, airline and/or train tickets, and any other documents that are crucial to the completion of the trip and my safe, hassle-free return home. I also take at least four passport-sized color photos. These are handy if you have to replace a passport, secure an international driver's license on short notice, or want to purchase a weekly or monthly Métro pass.

3. What's happening in Paris while you are there? The best source of events in Paris appears in two weekly magazines: *Pariscope: Une Semaine de Paris* and *l'Officiel des Spectacles*. They come out every Wednesday, cost about 4 francs, and list programs for the opera, theater, films, concerts, exhibits, special events, naughty night life, and weekly TV programs. There is even a list of swimming pools and interesting guided tours (given in French). Although the magazines are printed in French, a non-French speaker can quickly decipher the information given.

4. It isn't the washing that the hotels object to, it is the dripping. Dripping hangers of jeans, shirts, and underwear have ruined many carpets and stained many walls. If you must wash out a few things, please let them drip dry over the tub or sink. If you have a load to do, inquire about the nearest coin-operated laundromat. They are all over Paris and simple to use.

5. You will soon realize that Paris is a very noisy city both day and night. Something is always happening, making it heaven for night owls but a nightmare for insomniacs. Traffic, sirens, and voices magnify on the narrow streets, echoing and reechoing throughout the night. Street cleaning crews start their rounds at 0-dark-hundred, never thinking someone might still be sleeping—or wishing they could. If noise is a problem for you, ask for a room away from the street, in the back of the hotel, or facing the inner courtyard (*sur la cour*). For added insurance, buy or bring earplugs (*boules de quièss*).

6. French daylight savings time lasts from April until September. Depending on the time of year, France is six or seven hours ahead of Eastern Standard Time in the United States.

7. It is important to know that a *hôtel* is not always a hotel. The word *hôtel* has more than one meaning in French. Of course it means a lodging place for travelers. It also means a mansion or town house, like the Hôtel Lambert, or a large private home (a *hôtel particulier*). The city hall is the Hôtel de Ville; auctions are held at the Hôtel des Ventes; Hôtel des Postes refers to the general post office; and the Hôtel des Invalides, once a home for disabled war veterans, is now the most famous military museum in the world and the final resting place for Napoléon Bonaparte. Finally, if you are in the hospital, you are in a *Hôtel-Dieu*.

8. Budget-minded travelers always check with the airlines, or their travel agents, for package deals that include a greatly reduced airfare coupled with a car rental or a hotel at a fraction of the regular cost. TWA, American Airlines, and Delta have some of the better deals. If you are willing to take a chance and really lock yourself into a ticket that cannot be changed without an Act of Congress, then investigate the discount air ticketers who advertise on Sundays in most metropolitan newspapers. The fares are low, but the restrictions are many, so make sure you understand all the fine print and are able to live with it.

9. For museum-goers on a budget, there are now one-, three-, and five-day French passes that give unlimited access to more than 60 museums, including the Louvre and Musée d'Orsay. The pass is on sale in the museums, major Métro stations, and tourism offices in Paris, including the one at 127, Champs-Élysées. *La Carte* passes can also be purchased before leaving the United States through Challenges International, Inc., 10 East 21st Street, Suite 600, New York, NY 10010; 212-529-8484. The passes start at $16 if purchased here. The entrance fee for the Louvre is $4.50, so you can see that if many museums are on your list in Paris, this is a good deal. On Sundays all entry to government-run museums is free—but the crowds can be frightening.

How to Use
Cheap Sleeps in Paris

ABBREVIATIONS AND TERMS

The following abbreviations are used to denote which credit cards a hotel will accept:

American Express	AE
Diners Club	DC
MasterCard	MC
Visa	V

The following hotel-related terms will be helpful:

appartment	suite
chambre sur la cour	room on the courtyard
chambre simple	single room
chambre à deux/chambre double	double room
duplex	two-level suite
lit supplémentaire	extra bed
salon	sitting room
chambre avec eau courante	room with running water (washbasin only)
chambre avec cabinet de toilette	room with washbasin and bidet
chambre avec douche et WC	room with shower and toilet
chambre avec salle de bains	room with full bathroom including tub
baignoire	bathtub
couvertures	blankets
draps	sheets
oreiller	pillow
en sus	extra charge, as in *petit déjeuner, en sus*
faire la lessive	to do the laundry
petit déjeuner	breakfast
repasser	to iron

STARS

Hotels throughout France are controlled by a government rating system that ranks them from no stars to four-star deluxe. Every hotel must display prominently the number of stars it has.

A no-star hotel is mighty basic. A one-star hotel has minimum facilities. Two stars means a comfortable hotel with direct-dial phones in all rooms and an elevator in buildings of four or more stories. Three stars means a very comfortable hotel where all rooms have direct-dial phones and almost all have private plumbing. A four-star hotel is first class all the way, and a four-star deluxe is a virtual palace, with every service you could dream of.

Sometimes the number of stars in the lower categories bears little relationship to the quality of service or facilities you will find. Unfortunately, the stars on a hotel also do not correspond to the level of cleanliness or service. In short, you cannot always judge a hotel by its stars.

ACCOMMODATIONS: CHECKING IN

The lobby is usually one of the most attractive parts of a hotel, both because first impressions are important and because this is where the owner and manager spend their day. When you arrive at your hotel, ask to see your room. This is normal and expected practice in all hotels in France. If you are dissatisfied, ask to see another room. After approving the room, reconfirm the rate and whether or not you will be eating breakfast at the hotel. This advance work prevents any unpleasant surprises at checkout time.

In Paris, the hotel day begins and ends at noon. If you overstay, you could be charged the price of an extra day. If you are arriving before noon after a long international flight, the room might not be ready if the hotel is fully booked. If you think you might arrive after 6 P.M., be sure to notify the hotel; otherwise your room could be given away, even if you have a deposit.

In most cases, you pay for the room, not for the number of persons occupying it. Thus, if you are alone and occupy a triple, you will pay the triple price. Most rooms are for two, and the few singles tend to be tiny and on a top floor without much view, or along the back side facing a dreary wall. Most hotels have two kinds of double rooms: those with a double (*un grand lit*) and those with twin beds (*deux lits*). If you ask for a *double*, you will get a room with a double bed, so when reserving be sure to be specific about exactly what type of bed arrangements suit you.

RATES: PAYING THE BILL

Just like French restaurant menus, hotel rates and their number of stars must be posted, and the rates *must* include all taxes and services.

French hotel rates are no longer tightly controlled by the government, and, as a result, hotel prices are in a state of constant flux. The French government now gives special authorization for hotels to increase prices by a certain percentage twice a year. Many hotels offer different rates for different times of the year, getting what they can when they can, based on the law of supply and demand. It always makes good budget sense, therefore, to ask for a lower rate and, if possible, to go in the low season.

All rates listed in *Cheap Sleeps in Paris* are for full price and do not reflect any special deals. The rates indicate whether or not breakfast is extra or included, and, if included, whether or not the hotel will allow you to deduct it if not taken. While I have made every effort to be accurate on the rates, I cannot control changes or fluctuations of the dollar against the franc, so please be fully prepared to have the prices vary. All listings state which credit cards are accepted. In most Cheap Sleeps, payment is required one night in advance. Very few low-priced hotels or youth hostels take credit cards or personal checks; it is cash up front in French francs *only*. I have yet to see one of these hotels bend on this important point, so be prepared.

Hotel exchange rates are terrible. If you plan to pay your bill in francs, convert your money at a bank before checkout time (see "Currency Exchange," page 14). Before leaving the hotel, go over your bill carefully, question anything you don't understand, and get a receipt marked *paid* before leaving.

BREAKFAST

Almost all Parisian hotels serve a Continental breakfast consisting of coffee, tea , hot chocolate, bread, croissants, butter, and jam. Hotels stand to make as much as a 200 percent profit on this meal, so they naturally encourage their guests to take it at the hotel. If you want anything extra, it costs dearly and is usually not worth the extra francs. Many better hotels are now offering an all-you-can-eat buffet with cereals, yogurt, hard-boiled eggs, and fruit added to the standard Continental fare. Sometimes the buffet is worth the price, especially if you plan to skip lunch. If you are trying to save money, skip the hotel breakfast and join the locals standing at the corner café.

Unless otherwise noted, none of the hotels listed serve meals other than breakfast.

ENGLISH SPOKEN

All the listings in this book indicate whether English is spoken. Generally, if you can dust off a few French phrases, smile, and display good will, you will find that the hotel staff will prove to be astonishingly warm and friendly and go out of their way to serve you. If you don't speak any French and want to avoid the stress of trying to communicate, it is important that you know whether someone at the hotel speaks English. While it is fun to practice your high-school French, it is not fun to try to deal with a problem while struggling to speak it.

PARKING

Very few hotels have private parking. If a hotel does have it, it is stated in the Cheap Sleep listing, and so is the price per day. Public parking is well situated throughout the city, and finding a facility close to your hotel should not be too hard. The farthest you will have to walk is usually four or five blocks.

FACILITIES AND SERVICES

A brief summary at the end of each hotel listing states which facilities and services are offered. Of course, the better the hotel, the more offerings there will be.

NEAREST TOURIST ATTRACTIONS

Each hotel listing tells you whether the hotel is on the Right or Left Bank and gives nearest tourist attractions within a reasonable walking distance.

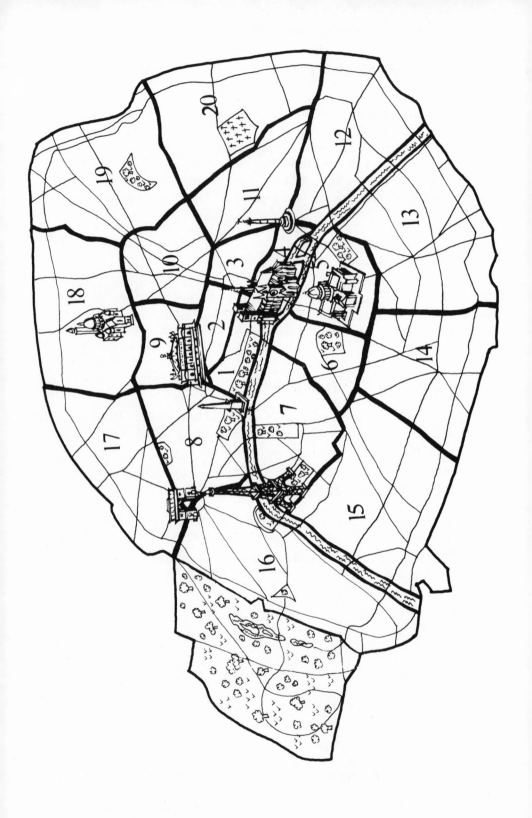

ARRONDISSEMENTS

Paris has more than 9 million inhabitants occupying 432 square miles. Despite these numbers, it is a very compact city, bound by a ring road (the *périphérique*) and divided into 20 districts known as arrondissements. In the late 19th century, Paris was reorganized and modernized by Baron Haussman, the farsighted planner who gave the city its wide boulevards, beautiful parks, and system of arrondissements that make up the city today. Each district has its own mayor, city hall, police station, and central post office. Knowing which arrondissement is which is the key to understanding Paris and quickly finding your way around. Starting with the first arrondissement, which is the district around the Louvre, the numbering of the districts goes clockwise in a rough spiral. From a visitor's standpoint, the arrondissements of greatest interest are the first through the eighth, although there are interesting things to see and do in the others as well. For instance, the Eiffel Tower is in the fifteenth; Montmartre occupies most of the eighteenth; and to see the latest artworks displayed in stunning, architecturally renovated lofts, or to attend a production at the controversial new Opéra, you will journey to the eleventh.

If you plan to be in Paris for more than one day, a necessary investment, and one that will last forever, is a copy of the *Plan de Paris par Arrondissement*. This Parisian "bible" offers a detailed map of each arrondissement, with a complete keyed street index, Métro and bus routes, tourist sites, churches, and other valuable information. It is available at newsstands and bookstores.

The arrondissement is noted in every address given in *Cheap Sleeps in Paris*. For example, (5th) indicates the fifth arrondissement. For mailing purposes, the Paris zip code is 750, followed by a two-digit number indicating the arrondissement (75001 for the first, 75004 for the fourth, and so on).

FIRST ARRONDISSEMENT

FIRST ARRONDISSEMENT
Right Bank: Conciergerie, Île de la Cité, Pont Neuf, Les Halles, Louvre, Palais de Justice, Palais Royal, Place Vendôme, Ste-Chapelle

The Tuileries Gardens and Louvre Museum are the cornerstones of this *quartier* and the center from which the arrondissement begins. Here you will find the rejuvenated Les Halles, the stunning Gothic masterpiece Ste-Chapelle with its magnificent red and blue stained-glass windows, and the Place Vendôme, a perfect example of classic French architecture. The palaces surrounding this square include famous jewelry stores, the Ministry of Justice, and the world-renowned Ritz Hotel, where room prices are within the budget of any average emir or Texas oil mogul.

HOTELS IN THE FIRST ARRONDISSEMENT
Grand Hôtel de Champagne ★★★
Hôtel de Lille **no stars**
Hôtel de Londres et de Stockholm ★★
Hôtel Henri IV **no stars**
Hôtel Molière ★★★
Hôtel Richelieu-Nazarin ★
Prince Albert Hôtel ★★
Timhôtel Louvre ★★
Tonic Hôtel les Halles ★★

Grand Hôtel de Champagne ★★★
17, rue Jean Lantier (1st)

TELEPHONE
42-36-60-00: toll free from U.S.: Utell International 1-800-44-UTELL
TELEX
215-955 F; 497-2677 (in the U.S.)
FAX
(1) 45-08-43-33
MÉTRO
Châtelet (exit Rivoli *nos impairs* [odd numbers]), Pont Neuf
CREDIT CARDS
AE, DC, MC, V

45 rooms, all with bath or shower and toilet

Hidden behind the sprawling Samaritaine department store, this family-owned hotel appeals to a tuned-in artistic crowd of French and German travelers. The location is A+ for exploring the Louvre, Beaubourg, and Forum des Halles, and is just across the Pont Neuf from Île de le Cité, Île St-Louis, St-Michel, and St-Germain-des-Prés.

Differing themes are carried out in the 45 rooms and three suites, with the interiors running the gamut from modern masculine to frankly feminine. Many of the rooms have hand-painted murals done by artists over the years (perhaps in lieu of a final payment?). Room No. 304 has a fanciful scene of Venice on the bathroom wall, and No. 302, one of my favorites, shows a pretty girl peeking through a cloud-filled sky. The unusual two-room suites may not appeal to everyone. However, if you like sunken bathtubs, platform beds, conversation pits with built-in sofas, lots of open space, and granite walls, one of these suites will be your answer. While the single and double rooms have all the modern amenities and are mercifully quiet for Paris, few have sparkling views, seating is sparse, some of the tiny closets are without doors, and luggage space is limited.

The management is very proud of their international breakfast buffet served downstairs every morning. Designed to appeal to lumberjack appetites, it includes fruits, juices, a wide variety of bread and rolls, several selections of meat and cheese, eggs and cereals. After this meal, you won't need to eat until dinnertime.

English Spoken: Yes

Facilities and Services: Bar, direct-dial phones, elevator, mini-bars in suites, TVs with international reception

Nearest Tourist Attractions (Right Bank): Forum des Halles, Beaubourg, Louvre, Île de la Cité, Île St-Louis, St-Michel, St-Germain-des-Prés, shopping at Samaritaine department store (which has the finest hardware department in France and is a do-it-yourselfer's heaven)

RATES
Single 550F, double 600F, triple 750F, suite 1,020F

BREAKFAST
Buffet 50F extra

Hôtel de Lille (no stars)
8, rue du Pélican (1st)

13 rooms, 3 with private shower, 10 with *no* shower and no toilet; *no* hall shower

No private toilets, no hall shower for rooms without showers, no English spoken, and, to date, no breakfast served in a hotel housed in a 13th-century building with five floors and no elevator. Who needs this? Seekers of a very Cheap Sleep near the Louvre do, and believe me, they stay here in droves. If you do decide to stay here, don't expect thick towels, a particularly helpful staff, mini-bars, TVs, or any other service or amenity. This is a Cheap Sleep thrill all

TELEPHONE
42-33-33-42

TELEX
None

FAX
None

MÉTRO
Palais-Royal, Louvre

CREDIT CARDS
None; cash only

RATES
Single 140F (no shower), double 250F (shower)

BREAKFAST
Not available, but planning to
serve it soon

right, but also a safe and clean one you can count on if all you need is a place to hang your hat and rest your weary head after a long day in Paris. Management hopes to start serving breakfast in the near future, but, frankly speaking, I wouldn't count on it.

English Spoken: None

Facilities and Services: None

Nearest Tourist Attractions (Right Bank): Louvre, Palais-Royal, Les Halles, Tuileries, shopping on Rue St-Honoré, Seine, Île de la Cité, Île St-Louis

Hôtel de Londres et de Stockholm ★★
300 rue Saint-Honoré (1st); entrance at 13, rue St-Roch

TELEPHONE
42-60-15-62
TELEX
210-259 F
FAX
(1) 42-60-16-00
MÉTRO
Tuileries, Pyramides
CREDIT CARDS
AE, DC, MC, V
RATES
Single 380–465F, double
550F, triple 635F, quad 700F
BREAKFAST
Continental, included; 25F can
be deducted per day if hotel is
informed you will not take
breakfast

30 rooms, all with bath, shower, and toilet

The family-owned Londres et de Stockholm is an old but well-patched budget choice in central Paris. Steep stairs lead off the street to the first-floor reception and lounge area, which is highlighted by a beautiful tropical fish tank. All the rooms are in different colors and are outfitted in nondescript modern and reproduction furnishings. Some of the halls slope, the toilet paper is square, and there is noise, but at these prices and in this location, you can't have it all. Lots of *Cheap Eats in Paris* restaurants are within an easy walk, and the area is pivotal for any visitor to Paris. Across the street is the Church of St-Roch, where Bonaparte fought the Royalists before he was Emperor Napoléon I. Within ten minutes you can be at the Louvre, admiring the Place Vendôme, jogging in the Jardin des Tuileries, or looking at the Chagall ceiling in the old Opéra.

English Spoken: Yes

Facilities and Services: Direct-dial phones, elevator to most floors, mini-bars, TVs

Nearest Tourist Attractions (Right Bank): Louvre, Tuileries, old Opéra, Place Vendôme, Seine, shopping on Rue St-Honoré

Hôtel Henri IV (no stars)
25, place Dauphine (1st)

TELEPHONE
43-54-44-53

22 rooms, none with bath, shower, or toilet; all with basins

Four hundred years ago King Henri IV's printing presses occupied this narrow town house on Île de la Cité's pretty Place Dauphine. Today, it is a 22-room hotel that has been touted in every budget guide to Paris and, as a result, has become a mecca for hardcore Cheap Sleepers and anyone else eager to experience a romantically threadbare hotel adventure in Paris. No one who knew the hotel thought it would ever happen, but a few years ago the Henri IV actually underwent a renovation of sorts. For starters, it was scrubbed and dusted, something it had desperately needed for years. Next, several rooms were painted and new linoleum was laid to replace the buckling and warped wooden floors that graced most rooms. Recently, a few rooms had new washbasins installed and new mattresses replaced a few of the tired and thin ones of times past. Despite these improvements, guests *must* continue to be philosophical about both the accommodations and the plumbing. The rooms, which passed their prime decades ago, could be a shock to some: the furniture looks like leftovers from a garage sale; the lighting is dim; only a bidet and basin come with each room; and the communal shower and toilets are reached via a steep, winding staircase in a dark and freezing-cold air shaft. On the other hand, it is so cheap, so perfectly located, so quiet, and the owners, M. and Mme Balitrand, are so friendly, that thousands of young-at-heart guests continue to flock here from around the world and reserve many months in advance.

English Spoken: Very Limited

Facilities and Services: None

Nearest Tourist Attractions: Île de la Cité, Île St-Louis, St-Michel, St-Germain-des-Prés, Latin Quarter, Left Bank, Louvre, Musée d'Orsay, Place Dauphine

TELEX
None

FAX
None

MÉTRO
Pont-Neuf

CREDIT CARDS
None; cash only

RATES
Single 90–120F, double 150–180F, extra bed 20F

BREAKFAST
Included (bread, butter, jam; coffee, tea, or chocolate)

Hôtel Molière ★★★

21, rue Moliére (1st)

32 rooms, all with bath or shower and toilet

You will have to look long and hard to top the overall comfort and services offered by the mid-city

TELEPHONE
42-96-22-01

TELEX
213-292 F

FAX
(1) 42-60-48-68
MÉTRO
Palais-Royal, Pyramides
CREDIT CARDS
AE, DC, MC, V
RATES
Single 390–550F, double 490–600F, suite 1,200F; extra bed 100F
BREAKFAST
Continental, 35F; buffet, 50F

Molière. A few years ago, this was a hotel to avoid. Not now. After a thorough redecorating project, and thanks to a smart and caring staff, it is definitely back on the map in a big way. The rooms, which are way above average in size and layout, are tastefully done in a rather formal French style. The amount of living space is exceptional; the views, even along the back, are pleasant; and the location puts the guests within walking distance of many of the tourist "musts" in Paris.

I could check right into No. 42 any day, with its rich brown velvet easy chairs, two wide-view windows, and nostalgic black and turquoise bathroom. Number 43, a mauve and pink single, is another favorite, and so is No. 46, with a large sitting room and a tango-sized bathroom.

English Spoken: Yes

Facilities and Services: Bar, direct-dial phones, elevator to 6th floor, hair dryers in rooms, mini-bars, TVs, and videos

Nearest Tourist Attractions (Right Bank): Old Opéra, Palais-Royal, Tuileries, Louvre, shopping on Rue St.-Honoré

Hôtel Richelieu-Nazarin ★
51, rue de Richelieu (1st)

TELEPHONE
42-97-46-20
TELEX
None
FAX
None
MÉTRO
Palais-Royal
CREDIT CARDS
None; cash only
RATES
Single 175F, double 200–385F, triple 385F, hall shower 10F, extra bed 70F
BREAKFAST
Continental, 25F

14 rooms, 12 with bath, shower, and toilet

Years ago the tiny Richelieu-Nazarin was a great Cheap Sleep; then it fell by the wayside due to poor upkeep and uncaring management. A new owner, M. Daniel, has changed all that, and now it can be again recommended for budgeters not in the market for fancy but looking for good value.

The entrance off the street is along a stone-walled, well-lighted hallway and up some steep steps to a reception area, which doubles as the breakfast room and lounge. Some of the simply done rooms are dark, and those on the street are noisy, but all are clean enough to please your mother-in-law and have adequate space. Long lines of regulars book way in advance, so if you want to stay here, please do the same.

English Spoken: Limited

Facilities and Services: Direct-dial phones, no elevator

Nearest Tourist Attractions (Right Bank): Palais-Royal, Louvre, Tuileries, shopping on Rue St-Honoré, Place Vendôme, old Opéra, Place de la Concorde

Prince Albert Hôtel ★★
5, rue Saint-Hyacinthe (1st)
33 rooms, all with bath or shower and toilet

Good-sized quiet rooms in central Paris for not too much money are what you can expect at the popular Prince Albert. The hotel consists of three side-by-side buildings joined by well-lighted hallways. The 33 bedrooms, which offer all the basics, plus individual safes, are furnished with a mixture of semi-antiques and period pieces. Within an interesting five- or ten-minute walk, you can be at the new Pyramid entrance to the Louvre, browsing along Rue St-Honoré, or standing at the Opéra Métro stop. Just around the corner is the Place du Marche St-Honoré, which has everything from a horse butcher and cheese shops to trendy wine bars and even trendier boutiques (see "Cheap Chic," page 163, for one of the best shoe stores in Paris). Many good restaurants in all price ranges are nearby (see *Cheap Eats in Paris*).

English Spoken: Yes

Facilities and Services: Direct-dial phones, elevator, mini-bars, private room safes, TVs

Nearest Tourist Attractions (Right Bank): Louvre, Tuileries, Palais-Royal, Place Vendôme, shopping on Rue St-Honoré

TELEPHONE
42-61-58-36

TELEX
220-227 F

FAX
(1) 42-60-04-06

MÉTRO
Tuileries, Pyramides

CREDIT CARDS
MC, V

RATES
Single 380–520F, double 535F, extra bed 275F

BREAKFAST
Continental, 33F

Timhôtels ★★ (1st, also 2nd, 8th, 13th, 14th, 15th, 18th)

Thanks to the Timhôtel chain, modern, budget-priced two-star hotels are flourishing in Paris. Some of the locations appeal more to French business travelers than they do to tourists, but all are listed here. This is the French version of Motel 6, with rooms cut out with the same cookie cutter, so don't expect to find old-world charm, period antiques, or individual touches. What you can expect are clean, contemporary rooms with private baths or showers, two free movies on video each day, decent service, and value for your money. As an added bonus, the eleventh night is free in any of the chain's hotels throughout France, and the ten nights leading up to it do not have to be consecutive, or spent in any one particular Timhôtel. Children under 12 may stay free in their parents' room. Some of the hotels have rooms for the handicapped, saunas, and conference rooms.

For ease in booking any Timhôtel, contact the central reservations center:
Telephone: 42-96-28-28
Telex: 215-350 F
Fax: (1) 40-20-96-98
If you prefer, you may deal directly with each hotel. In that case, see the individual specifications for each location.

Timhôtel Louvre ★★
4, rue Croix-des-Petits-Champs (1st)

56 rooms, all with bath or shower and toilet

See immediately above for general information on all the Timhôtels.

A note of caution: Until 1994, a massive, earshattering construction project will be underway directly across from this hotel. Work hours are Monday through Friday from 8 A.M. to 7 P.M. Unless you are there on a Saturday or Sunday, or noise isn't a problem, I suggest you request a room as far away from the construction noise as possible.

English Spoken: Yes

Facilities and Services: Bar, direct-dial phones, elevator, rooms for the handicapped, TVs with international reception, radios, videos

Nearest Tourist Attractions (Right Bank): Tuileries, Louvre, Palais-Royal, Concorde, Forum des Halles, Beaubourg

TELEPHONE
42-60-34-86
TELEX
216-405 F
FAX
(1) 42-60-05-39
MÉTRO
Palais-Royal
CREDIT CARDS
AE, DC, MC, V
RATES
Single 400F, double 495–520F, triple 520–650F, quad 770F
BREAKFAST
Continental; 32F downstairs, 45F served in room

Tonic Hôtel les Halles ★★
12–14, rue du Roule (1st)
38 rooms, 28 with bath, shower, and toilet

Physical-fitness buffs who stay in the new section of the Tonic Hôtel les Halles can keep themselves in top shape during their visit to the City of Light. The pastel rooms are nothing fancy, but they do include luggage racks, mirrored wardrobes, and double-paned windows to keep out street noise. While the rooms may seem basic to some, everyone will fall in love with the white-tiled bathrooms, which have either a built-in steam bath, a Jacuzzi in the bathtub, or a pulsating shower massager to ease away the aches and pains of daily tourist safaris through Paris. Those on tighter budgets will want to reserve one of the simpler rooms, which are true bargains for this part of Paris, especially during the low season. No matter where your room is, if you are a morning jogger or walker, it is only a hop, skip, and a jump to join fellow exercisers in the Tuileries or along the banks of the Seine. The hotel is also well located from a sightseeing standpoint, and there are many good restaurants within easy walking distance (see *Cheap Eats in Paris*).

English Spoken: Yes

Facilities and Services: None in simple rooms. In all other rooms: Bar, direct-dial phones, elevator, mini-bars, TVs with international reception, hair dryers, shower massagers or steam baths, some Jacuzzis

Nearest Tourist Attractions (Right Bank): Louvre, Tuileries, Seine, Palais-Royal, Forum des Halles, Île de la Cité, Île St-Louis, St-Michel

TELEPHONE
42-33-00-71

TELEX
205-340 Taranne

FAX
(1) 40-26-06-86 (Les Halles)

MÉTRO
Louvre, Châtelet

CREDIT CARDS
AE, DC, MC, V

RATES
Simple rooms in old part of hotel (no TV, mini-bar, or elevator): Low season: Single or double 210F (washbasin only)–315F, (shower and toilet); high season: Single or double 210F (washbasin only)–400F (shower and toilet); shower 17F per person. Upgraded rooms with all facilities: Low season: Single or double 475–520F, triple 580F; high season: Single or double 519–580F, triple 685F

BREAKFAST
Buffet, 30F

SECOND ARRONDISSEMENT

The second is known as the area of finance (around the stock exchange, or Bourse) and the press. It makes up for its small size with the beautiful Victorian shopping *passages* and the many boutiques around Place des Victoires.

SECOND ARRONDISSEMENT
Right Bank: Bibliothèque Nationale, Bourse, Cognacq-Jay Museum, *passages*, Place des Victoires

HOTELS IN THE SECOND ARRONDISSMENT
Grand Hôtel de Malte ★★★
Hôtel Favart ★★★
Hôtel Gaillon Opéra ★★★
Timhôtel Bourse ★★

Grand Hôtel de Malte ★★★
63, rue de Richelieu (2nd)

TELEPHONE
42-96-58-06

TELEX
Hotmalt 216-177 F

FAX
(1) 42-86-88-19

MÉTRO
Bourse, Palais-Royal, Pyramides

CREDIT CARDS
AE, DC, MC, V

RATES
Single 495F, double 690F, triple 990F, suite or quad 1,320F; extra bed 175F

BREAKFAST
Continental with juice and cheese; 55F in room, 50F downstairs

59 rooms, all with bath or shower and toilet

In an area appealing to French business travelers and other Europeans, the Grand Hôtel de Malte is one of the better hotels in its price category in this area. The rich past of the hotel dates back to 1797, when it was home to the first American ministers serving in France. When I checked the hotel a few years ago, it fell into the "Oh, no!" category, and it was clear not much had been done to upgrade it since the turn of the century. Since then, miracles have taken place. The Legers, an attractive couple who inherited the hotel from Mme Leger's grandparents, have lifted it out of the doldrums to reflect their modern approach to the hotel business. In restoring the hotel, they kept the magnificent balconied facade, the wide mezzanines, the high double French windows, the beautiful brass-and-iron-grillwork stairway, and many pieces of antique furniture. Recently, they added a glorious heated garden breakfast room, modernized the bathrooms, and installed firm mattresses and new carpeting.

A major advantage, from a guest's point of view, is the size of the rooms. Even the smallest singles have luggage racks, writing desks, and full-length mirrors. The larger rooms have an entryway, high ceilings, built-in drawers in the closets, and ample space to spread out and settle in. Another advantage is that few rooms, even on the back, have those grim inner courtyard views. The drawbacks include square "sandy" toilet paper, some street-side noise, and steep winding staircases in the two-level suites.

English Spoken: Yes

Facilities and Services: Bar, conference room, direct-dial phones, hair dryers, TVs

Nearest Tourist Attractions (Right Bank): Old Opéra, Palais-Royal, Louvre, Bibliotèque Nationale, Comédie Française

Hôtel Favart ★★★
5, rue Marivaux (2nd)
38 rooms, all with bath or shower and toilet

During the summer of 1824, the painter Françisco Goya lived at the Favart. Now this old-fashioned hotel appeals to a faithful British crowd who appreciate getting good value for their hotel pound. The roomy lobby with its faux marble columns and fringed red and black velvet chairs has a certain faded elegance and character that suggest better times. The bedrooms are definitely not for those who like Louis XV decor, but are all clean and have two chairs, a writing table with decent lighting, and a large bathroom. The hotel is located across the street from the Opéra Comique and near the old Opéra and the Comedie Française. Good Métro and bus connections are within a five-minute walk, and in only ten or fifteen, you can be shopping at Galeries Lafayette or browsing through Au Printemps.

English Spoken: Yes

Facilities and Services: Direct-dial phones, hair dryers, mini-bars, TVs

Nearest Tourist Attractions (Right Bank): Old Opéra, Comedie Française, shopping at Galeries Lafayette and Au Printemps, *grandes boulevards*

TELEPHONE
42-97-59-83

TELEX
213-126 F

FAX
(1) 40-15-95-58

MÉTRO
4-Septembre

CREDIT CARDS
AE, DC, MC, V

RATES
Single 480F, double 580F, triple 650F, quad 735F

BREAKFAST
Continental, 20F; included, but can be deducted

Hôtel Gaillon Opéra ★★★
9, rue Gaillon (2nd)
26 rooms, all with bath or shower and toilet

Fresh flowers, antiques, exposed beams, stone walls, and tapestry-covered furniture set the Gaillon Opéra apart from its cool modern counterparts in this neighborhood around the Opéra. The compact rooms are always in perfect order and have the creature comforts most people deem necessary: a modern bathroom with plenty of towels and a hair dryer, and pleasing room decor with luggage racks, adequate closet space, firm mattresses, comfortable seating, and

TELEPHONE
47-42-47-74; toll free in the U.S. and Canada: 800-528-1234

TELEX
215-716 F

FAX
(1) 47-42-01-23

MÉTRO
Opéra

CREDIT CARDS
AE, DC, MC , V

RATES
Single 500–600F, double 700F, triple 800F, quad 900F
BREAKFAST
Continental, 25F; included, but can be deducted

good lighting. The management, under the direction of Denise Wolecki, is conscientious and concerned about guests' welfare. Both French- and English-language newspapers are available for skimming while enjoying a second café au lait and croissant in the morning.

English Spoken: Yes

Facilities and Services: Bar, direct-dial phones, elevator, hair dryers, mini-bars, room safes, room service for light snacks, TVs

Nearest Tourist Attractions (Right Bank): Old Opéra, shopping at Place des Victoires, Place Vendôme

TELEPHONE
42-61-53-90
TELEX
214-488 F
FAX
(1) 42-60-05-39
MÉTRO
Bourse
RATES
Single 493F, double 478–510F; extra bed 130F
BREAKFAST
Continental; 35F downstairs, 48F served in rooms

Timhôtel Bourse ★★
3, rue de la Banque (2nd)

See page 35 for general information on all the Timhôtels.

English Spoken: Yes

Facilities and Services: Direct-dial phones, elevator, billiards, TVs, videos, radios

Nearest Tourist Attractions (Right Bank): old Opéra, Louvre, Tuileries, Palais-Royal, Concorde

THIRD ARRONDISSEMENT

THIRD ARRONDISSEMENT
Right Bank: Carnavalet Museum (City of Paris museum), French National Archives, Marais, Picasso Museum

This area includes the northern parts of the revitalized Marais, which 30 years ago was one of the worst slums in Paris. Today the magnificent 17th-century buildings have been turned into museums, the most famous of which is the Picasso Museum.

HOTELS IN THE THIRD ARRONDISSEMENT
Hôtel des Chevaliers ★★★
Hôtel du Chancelier Boucherat **no stars**
Hôtel du Marais ★★

Hôtel des Chevaliers ★★★
30, rue de Turenne (3rd)
24 rooms, all with bath or shower and toilet

A recent and extensive renovation project has completely transformed this once seedy spot into a charming hotel. The rooms aren't large, but the great location near the Picasso Museum and on the edge of the vibrant Marais puts it on the list of desirable Cheap Sleeps.

The smartly done pastel-colored rooms have fabric-covered walls and are soundproofed by double-paned windows. The bathrooms are tiny but impeccably modern. The downstairs breakfast room is fashioned from the original 17th-century *cave*, with the original water well still in one corner. Nicely upholstered chairs are placed around well-lighted tables where breakfast is served on individual trays. The management is outgoing and friendly, and repeat guests are many.

English Spoken: Yes

Facilities and Services: Direct-dial phones, elevator to all but 5th floor, hair dryers, mini-bars, room safes, TVs with international reception

Nearest Tourist Attractions (Right Bank): Marais, Place des Vosges, Picasso Museum, Bastille

TELEPHONE
42-72-73-47

TELEX
211-544 F HOT CHEV

FAX
(1) 42-72-54-10

MÉTRO
Bastille, Chemin-Vert, St-Paul

CREDIT CARDS
AE, DC, MC, V

RATES
1 or 2 persons 540–560F

BREAKFAST
Continental, 35F

Hôtel du Chancelier Boucherat (no stars)
110, rue du Turenne (3rd)

39 rooms, 17 with bath or shower and toilet

The Boucherat is an address where Cheap Sleepers will find tiny rooms, creaky furniture, and intimidating wallpaper. In addition, the towels are thin, the floors tend to slope, and some of the carpets covering them are threadbare. As you can see, management spares no effort in cutting corners in order to keep the prices down at the rock-bottom level. From a more positive standpoint, almost all of the beds are amazingly good, and the hall toilets and showers are clean. There is also a pretty garden–breakfast area where guests gather to compare cheap travel tips gleaned from years of surviving on the very edge of things. The international budget-minded clientele books months in advance, and you must too, if you want to stay here.

English Spoken: No

TELEPHONE
42-72-86-83

TELEX
None

FAX
None

MÉTRO
Filles-du-Calvaire

CREDIT CARDS
MC, V

RATES
Single 165F, double 190–310F, triple 275–330F, quad 385F; hall shower 15F

BREAKFAST
Continental (no croissants), 22F

Facilities and Services: Direct-dial phones, no elevator

Nearest Tourist Attractions (Right Bank): Everything a long walk away; must use bus or Métro

Hôtel du Marais ★★
2 bis, rue Commines (3rd)
39 rooms, all with bath or shower and toilet

TELEPHONE
48-87-78-27

TELEX
260-717 F

FAX
(1) 48-87-09-01

MÉTRO
Filles du Calvaire, St-Sebastien
Froissart

CREDIT CARDS
AE, DC, MC, V

RATES
Single 320F, double 352–462F

BREAKFAST
Continental, 30F

Monsieur and Madame Benattia's Hôtel du Marais has staged a great comeback at the end of an impressive two-year remodeling project. In keeping with the spirit of the area near the Place des Vosges, they kept the old wooden ceilings, stone walls, and red-tiled floors in the downstairs area and in the separate sitting room off the lobby. A tiny elevator geared to one thin person and one small suitcase carries guests to simple, bandbox-sized rooms. Space is tight but used judiciously, especially in the bathrooms, which have been carved out of whatever space the carpenter could find. The rooms are done in light colors with wicker accessories and built-in closets. No one could ever call them glamorous, but they are functional provided you plan a short stay and have little baggage.

English Spoken: Yes

Facilities and Services: Direct-dial phone, elevator, mini-bars, some room safes, TVs

Nearest Tourist Attractions (Right Bank): Marais, Picasso Museum, Place des Vosges

FOURTH ARRONDISSEMENT

FOURTH ARRONDISSEMENT
Right Bank: Centre Georges Pompidou (Beaubourg), Hôtel-de-Ville (City Hall), Île St-Louis, Jewish Quarter, Maison de Victor Hugo, continuation of the Marais, Notre-Dame, Place des Vosges

This arrondissement stretches from the Marais through the ancient Jewish quarter on the Rue des Rosiers to the islands in the middle of the Seine. It is an area perfectly suited to exploring on foot, lending itself to discovery at almost every turn. Its immense charm comes from a wonderful mixture of past and present. The focal point of the area is Notre-Dame Cathedral, the geographical and spiritual heart of France. The Île St-Louis, behind the cathedral, is considered by many to be one of the most desirable, and admittedly expensive, places to reside in Paris. The island is a capsule of all that is Paris, with interesting shops, art galleries, boutiques, baroque mansions, and lovely views along its *quais*. Also in this arrondissement is the Place des Vosges and the Centre George Pompidou (Beaubourg), which logs more visitors each year than the Eiffel Tower.

HOTELS IN THE FOURTH ARRONDISSEMENT
Castex Hôtel ★
Grand Hôtel Jeanne d'Arc ★★
Grand Hôtel Malher ★
Hôtel Bastille Speria ★★★
Hôtel de la Bretonnerie ★★★
Hôtel de la Place des Vosges ★★
Hôtel de Lutèce ★★★
Hôtel des Deux-Îles ★★★
Hôtel Saint-Louis ★★
Hôtel Saint-Merry ★★★
Hôtel Saint-Paul le Marais ★★★

Castex Hôtel ★
5, rue Castex (4th)
24 rooms, all with bath or shower and toilet

The Castex used to be my favorite faded no-star hotel on the Right Bank. A few years ago, the Bouchand family, who have owned the hotel since 1929, decided to modernize. In the process, they tossed out all the old, brought in the new and gained a star. Now it is a plain-as-a-pin, very clean, and well-maintained Cheap Sleep done in French Motel Moderne, with none of its former attic-chic character left. Of course the location near the Bastille, which is an "in" spot for animated night life and anything else on the wild side, has not changed. The morning coffee and hot chocolate are still served piping hot, and the owners continue to be sweet and friendly. Even though in turning over a new leaf the hotel lost its funky charm, it is still a great Cheap Sleep.

English Spoken: Yes, if the son is there

Facilities and Services: Direct-dial phones, no elevator

TELEPHONE
42-72-31-52

TELEX
None

FAX
(1) 42-72-57-91

MÉTRO
Bastille

CREDIT CARDS
MC, V

RATES
Single 190–245F, double 250–300F, triple 390F

BREAKFAST
Continental, 30F

Nearest Tourist Attractions (Right Bank): Bastille, new Opéra, Marais, Seine, Île de la Cité, Île St-Louis, St-Germain-des-Prés

Grand Hôtel Jeanne d'Arc ★★
3, rue de Jarente (4th)

TELEPHONE
48-87-62-11

TELEX
None

FAX
None

MÉTRO
St-Paul

CREDIT CARDS
MC, V

RATES
1 or 2 persons
300–370F, 3
persons 420F, 4
persons 470F

BREAKFAST
Continental, 30F

37 rooms, all with bath or shower and toilet

Sitting on a relatively quiet street that leads into the Marais, the Grand Hôtel Jeanne d'Arc reminds me of *grand'mère's* sitting room, with its lace doilies, ferns and flowers everywhere, and bric-a-brac galore. Discovered long ago by astute Cheap Sleepers, the hotel offers spotless rooms with a minimum of snags and tears in the furnishings. I think the best rooms are on the first floor. No. 11 or 12 is a good bet if there are two of you, and if there are four, No. 15 is a good choice. The no-nonsense owners rule the roost from behind a little desk off the entrance, seeing to it that all guests are well taken care of. Repeat customers comprise the bulk of the clientele, which makes advance reservations, accompanied with a one-night deposit, mandatory at least six weeks in advance.

English Spoken: Limited

Facilities and Services: Direct-dial phones, elevator, TVs with international reception

Nearest Tourist Attractions (Right Bank): Marais, Place des Vosges, Picasso Museum, Bastille, new Opéra

Grand Hôtel Malher ★
5, rue Malher (4th)

TELEPHONE
42-72-60-92

TELEX
None

FAX
(1) 42-72-25-37

MÉTRO
St-Paul

CREDIT CARDS
None; cash only

36 rooms, 10 with bath or shower and toilet

For more than 50 years, the Fossiez family has been running this hardcore Cheap Sleep in the Marais. You can overlook the fact that you have to hike up stairs to get to your room, which is done in shades of orange chenille. Never mind that these bedchambers are faded and worn, that the furniture has its share of nicks and dents, and that the beds are sagging. In addition, the towels are thin and the toilet paper the square and scratchy variety. Let's look on the bright side. The location puts you within walking distance of the Place des Vosges, the islands, the Left Bank, and all the action in and around Les Halles and the Bastille. The owners are *sympa*, and so are the student and backpacker guests who appreciate this Cheap Sleep as one of the better one-star deals in the fourth arrondissement. Reservations are necessary at least three weeks in advance, and must be accompanied with a deposit check in French francs.

English Spoken: No

Facilities and Services: Direct-dial phones, no elevator

Nearest Tourist Attractions (Right Bank): Place des Vosges, Picasso Museum, Île de la Cité, Île St-Louis, Left Bank, St-Germain-des-Prés, Les Halles, Bastille, new Opéra

RATES
1 or 2 persons 135–310F, 3 persons 340F; hall shower 15F

BREAKFAST
Continental (no croissants), 20F

Hôtel Bastille Speria ★★★
1, rue de la Bastille (4th)

42 rooms, all with bath or shower and toilet

With the opening of the new Opéra, along with many galleries, new wave boutiques, trendy restaurants, and hot night spots throughout the *quartier*, the Bastille is one of the most fashionable places to be seen in Paris today. Visitors longing to be in the center of all this action can stay at the Bastille Speria, which is next to the famed brasserie Bofinger (see *Cheap Eats in Paris*, page 62) and only a few yards from the Place de la Bastille. The interior of the hotel was renovated from top to bottom in the late 1980s and continues to be impressively maintained. The rooms have clean, uncluttered lines and are decorated in soft grays and forest greens with contemporary furnishings. The modern but comfortable breakfast area and lounge downstairs have the same trim lines.

English Spoken: Yes

Facilities and Services: Direct-dial phones, elevator, hair dryers, mini-bars, TVs with international reception

Nearest Tourist Attractions (Right Bank): New Opéra, Bastille, Place des Vosges, Marais, Picasso Museum

TELEPHONE
42-72-04-01

TELEX
214-327 F

FAX
(1) 42-72-56-38

MÉTRO
Bastille

CREDIT CARDS
AE, DC, MC, V

RATES
Single 475–510F, double 510–600F, triple 730F; extra bed 70F

BREAKFAST
Continental, 40F

Hôtel de la Bretonnerie ★★★
22, rue Sainte-Croix-de-la-Bretonnerie (4th)

TELEPHONE
48-87-77-63

TELEX
None

FAX
(1) 42-77-26-78

MÉTRO
Hôtel-de-Ville

CREDIT CARDS
MC, V

RATES
1 or 2 persons 530–620F,
duplex 750F, suite 880F

BREAKFAST
Continental, 45F

31 rooms, all with bath or shower and toilet

A stay in this captivating hotel will make you feel like an inhabitant of old-world Paris. Set in a restored 17th-century town house in the heart of the picturesque Marais, it is just minutes from Beaubourg (Centre Georges Pompidou), Place des Vosges, the Picasso Museum, the banks of the Seine, and Notre-Dame.

Quality and taste are evident throughout the rooms, which are attractively furnished in Louis XIII style. For a very special treat, request No. 7, 17, 19, or 35. Set under medieval beams, No. 35 is magnificently done in soft mauve tones and has lovely antiques. It consists of a bedroom, a separate sitting room, and one of the most beautiful three-star marble baths in Paris. High praise goes to the owners, M. and Mme Sagot, for providing a warm and friendly welcome to their many returning guests, who rightfully consider this to be one of the best small hotels in Paris.

English Spoken: Yes

Facilities and Services: Bar, direct-dial phones, elevator, TVs

Nearest Tourist Attractions (Left Bank): Place des Vosges, Bastille, new Opéra, Beaubourg, Forum des Halles, Marais, Picasso Museum, Seine, Île de la Cité, Île St-Louis

Hôtel de la Place des Vosges ★★
12, rue de Birague (4th)

TELEPHONE
42-72-60-46

TELEX
None

FAX
(1) 42-72-02-64

MÉTRO
St-Paul, Bastille

CREDIT CARDS
AE, DC, MC, V

RATES
Single 280F, double 380F,
large double 414F

16 rooms, all with bath or shower and toilet

A vigorous transformation project more than a decade ago turned this ancient little hotel into an eye-catching choice on the edge of the beautiful Place des Vosges, the oldest square in Paris and one that is steeped in the history of the city. Victor Hugo, Cardinal Richelieu, and Madame de Sévigné all lived on this square, and the present inhabitants of the area are no less influential, wealthy, or powerful. The setting puts the visitor in the heart of the Marais and within easy walking distance of the Picasso Museum and the rapidly developing area around Bastille and the new Opéra. It is also close to amusing night spots and many outstanding restaurants (see *Cheap Eats in Paris*).

BREAKFAST
Continental, 35F

In the hotel restoration, the owners displayed faithful attention to detail and maintained the architectural past of the building by keeping the original beamed ceilings, wood-paneled walls, and tapestries. Like the hotel, the prices are small, and so are most of the 16 simply done rooms. Miniscule bathrooms and closets complement the luggage space, which is almost nil. If you don't mind tiny, this is a delightful and popular hotel in a fascinating part of Paris.

English Spoken: Yes

Facilities and Services: Direct-dial phones, elevator from the second floor

Nearest Tourist Attractions (Right Bank): Place des Vosges, Marais, Picasso Museum, Bastille, new Opéra, Seine, Île de la Cité, Île St-Louis

Hôtel de Lutèce ★★★
65, rue Saint-Louis-en-l'Île (4th)

23 rooms, all with bath or shower and toilet

The Île St-Louis is a small island in the middle of the Seine, six blocks long and two blocks wide. Every day, and especially on weekends, crowds of tourists and Parisians surge down the main street, browsing through the boutiques and art galleries, stopping for an ice cream at the famed Berthillon, or enjoying lunch or dinner at one of the many good restaurants (see *Cheap Eats in Paris*).

Lovers of this unique part of Paris check into either the Lutèce or the Deux Îles (see below), both owned by husband-and-wife team Roland and Elisabeth Buffat. The rooms at the Lutèce are not large by any standards, but they have just been redecorated and have the requisite exposed beams, provincial prints, and pretty views over the rooftops (if you are lucky and secure a top-floor room facing front). Stepping inside from the island's main street, you are welcomed by bouquets of fresh flowers and a

TELEPHONE
43-26-23-52

TELEX
None

FAX
(1) 43-29-60-25

MÉTRO
Pont-Marie

CREDIT CARDS
None; cash only

RATES
Single 580F, double 685F, triple 935F

BREAKFAST
Continental, 40F

large stone fireplace surrounded by soft couches and armchairs. The hotel exudes charm from top to bottom and is booked months ahead, so you should reserve as far in advance as possible.

English Spoken: Yes

Facilities and Services: Direct-dial phones, elevator, hair dryer, radio, TVs

Nearest Tourist Attractions: Île St-Louis, Île de la Cité, St-Germain-des-Prés, St-Michel, Bastille, Place des Vosges

Hôtel des Deux-Îles ★★★
59, rue Saint-Louis-en-l'Île (4th)
17 rooms, all with bath or shower and toilet

TELEPHONE
43-26-13-35

TELEX
None

FAX
(1) 43-29-60-25

MÉTRO
Pont-Marie

CREDIT CARDS
None; cash only

RATES
Single 580F, double 680F

BREAKFAST
Continental, 45F

This beautiful 17th-century mansion has been written about in virtually every guidebook, and it is easy to see why. Owned and lovingly restored by decorator Roland Buffat and his charming wife, it shows their touches at every turn, from the lobby with its atrium garden to the Louis XIV tiled bathrooms. The snug hotel bar has a roaring fireplace, an open library corner, and hidden nooks with soft overstuffed sofas, making it a perfect place for a romantic rendezvous on a cold winter evening. The rooms, where the very essence of Paris can be viewed from the top-floor windows, are very small, but nicely decorated with provincial prints, fabric wall treatments, and bamboo furniture. All this is on the Île St-Louis, putting the visitor near its many wonderful restaurants (see *Cheap Eats in Paris*), small galleries, and interesting shops, and only inches from Notre-Dame and all the Left Bank has to offer.

English Spoken: Yes

Facilities and Services: Bar, direct-dial phones, elevator, hair dryers, TVs

Nearest Tourist Attractions: Île St-Louis, Île de la Cité, Latin Quarter, St-Michel, St-Germain-des-Prés, Seine, Marais, Picasso Museum, Place des Vosges, Bastille, new Opéra

Hôtel Saint-Louis ★★
75, rue Saint-Louis-en-l'Île (4th)
21 rooms, all with bath or shower and toilet

To capture the excitement of being in Paris, stay on the Île St-Louis—but be forewarned, you may never want to leave!

Many people like being on the island because they are steps from the cultural cluster of Notre-Dame, Ste-Chapelle, and the Conciergerie; within walking distance to the Marais; and close to the developing area around Bastille. Only a few feel isolated and frustrated by its narrow streets, weekend crowds, and lack of easy parking. Personally, I love it, but I am biased because this is where I lived the first year I spent in Paris.

At the Hôtel Saint-Louis, guests are warmly greeted in a flower-filled Louis XII lobby. The rooms have a cozy ambience created by the use of exposed wood and a scattering of antiques. My favorite rooms are on the fourth and fifth floors, with photogenic views over the island's rooftops. Number 52 is a top-floor room tucked under the eaves with a balcony off the bedroom and bathroom where you can glimpse a corner of the Seine.

English Spoken: Yes

Facilities and Services: Direct-dial phones, elevator

Nearest Tourist Attractions: Île St-Louis, Île de la Cité, Left Bank, St-Germain-des-Prés, St-Michel, Latin Quarter, Marais, Palace des Vosges, Picasso Museum, Bastille, new Opéra

TELEPHONE
46-34-04-80

TELEX
None

FAX
(1) 46-34-02-13

MÉTRO
Pont-Marie

CREDIT CARDS
None; cash only

RATES
1 or 2 persons 570–670F, extra bed 190F

BREAKFAST
Continental, 45F

Hôtel Saint-Merry ★★★
78, rue de la Verrerie (4th)
12 rooms, 8 with bath or shower and toilet

The former presbytery of the 17th-century Gothic church of St-Merry is now the most unusual hotel in Paris. It is the labor of love of owner M. Crabbe, who for more than 30 years has been working with a full-time carpenter to create a true Gothic masterpiece. His immense pride in his achievement is well deserved, and the results are spectacular.

The entrance to the hotel is through a short hallway with exposed beams and stone steps leading up to

TELEPHONE
42-78-14-15

TELEX
None

FAX
(1) 40-29-06-82

MÉTRO
Châtelet, Hôtel-de-Ville

CREDIT CARDS
None; cash only

RATES
1 or 2 persons 390–1,000F (no
two rooms alike; prices vary
according to plumbing and
how Gothic room is).

BREAKFAST
Continental, 45F

the lobby and reception area. Each room in the hotel is different and showcases a wonderful collection of authentic Gothic church and castle memorabilia mixed with custom-made pieces. All the back rooms share a common wall with the church, and wherever possible this stone wall has been kept visible. One room contains a carved stone flying buttress, flowing from the floor to the ceiling over the bed. Others have rough red tiles from the Château de l'Angeres in the Loire Valley, hand-carved mahogany pews, or converted confessionals serving as headboards. All of the windows in the hotel are stained glass, and the balcony rails still bear the St-Merry church crest.

Warning: Located on a pedestrian walkway, the hotel is accessible by car or taxi *only* to the determined.

English Spoken: Yes

Facilities and Services: Direct-dial phones, no elevator

Nearest Tourist Attractions (Right Bank): You will be staying in one! Beaubourg, Forum des Halles, Marais, Seine, Île de la Cité, Île St-Louis, St-Germain-des-Prés. Don't miss the St-Merry church adjoining the hotel. It has a beautiful choir and the oldest church bell in Paris, cast in 1331.

Hôtel Saint-Paul le Marais ★★★
8, rue de Sévigné (4th)

27 rooms, all with bath or shower and toilet

TELEPHONE
48-04-97-27

TELEX
None

FAX
(1) 48-87-37-04

MÉTRO
St-Paul

CREDIT CARDS
AE, DC, MC, V

RATES
Single 480F, double 580F,
triple 750F; extra bed 100F

BREAKFAST
Continental, 40F

A few years ago, Michelle Legrand sold her dress boutique a few blocks away and bought this crumbling old building. She then transformed it into an appealing 27-room hotel offering uniformly decorated and well-appointed rooms with beams, sunshine, and soothing color schemes in mauve, blue, gray, and yellow.

Because the building is centuries old, the rooms are small, with closet and luggage space at a premium. The white-tiled baths are also on the small side, but fluffy towels and the latest in fixtures make up for this. Morning coffee, croissants, and fresh fruits are served in an old stone cellar brightened by vases of fresh flowers, antiqued wooden furniture, and peach-tapestry-upholstered chairs. In the summer, breakfast is served in a bricked garden framed by flowering planter boxes.

English Spoken: Yes

Facilities and Services: Bar, conference room, direct-dial phones, elevator, private room safes, TVs, private hotel parking

Nearest Tourist Attractions (Right Bank): Place des Vosges, Picasso Museum, Bastille, Marais, Île de la Cité, Île St-Louis, St-Germain-des-Prés, Left Bank

FIFTH ARRONDISSEMENT

The fifth, known as the Latin Quarter, stretches from the colorful *marché* on Rue Mouffetard to the dome of the Panthéon, through the botanical wonders of the Jardin des Plantes to the area around the Sorbonne. This ancient, interesting, and exhilarating part of Paris is crisscrossed with networks of narrow, curved streets lined on both sides with bookshops, restaurants, and cafés that surge with 24-hour action. It is youthful, cosmopolitan, bohemian, and fun. Even though St-Michel has lost its penniless chic, it is still the soul of the Latin Quarter. Crowds of all ages and types gather daily around the St-Michel fountain to flirt, eat, drink, argue, and watch the sidewalk entertainers perform.

FIFTH ARRONDISSEMENT
Left Bank: Cluny Museum, Jardin des Plantes, Latin Quarter, Rue Mouffetard, Panthéon, Sorbonne

HOTELS IN THE FIFTH ARRONDISSEMENT
Familia Hôtel ★★
Grand Hôtel de Lima ★★
Grand Hôtel Oriental ★
Hôtel Agora St-Germain ★★★
Hôtel Claude Bernard ★★★
Hôtel de la Sorbonne ★★
Hôtel des Allies ★
Hôtel des Grandes Écoles ★★
Hôtel des Grands Hommes ★★★
Hôtel des 3 Collèges ★★
Hôtel du Collège de France ★★
Hôtel du Panthéon ★★★

Hôtel Esmeralda ★★
Hôtel le Colbert ★★★
Hôtel Gay-Lussac ★
Hôtel Marignan ★
Le Jardin de Cluny ★★★
Le Jardin des Plantes ★★
Le Notre Dame Hôtel ★★★
Hôtel Parc Saint-Séverin ★★★
Select Hotel ★★★

Familia Hôtel ★★
11, rue des Écoles (5th)

TELEPHONE
43-54-55-27

TELEX
260-660 F

FAX
(1) 43-29-61-77

MÉTRO
Jussieu, Cardinal-Lemoine,
Maubert-Mutualité

CREDIT CARDS
DC, MC, V

RATES
Single 340–450F, double 380–450F, triple 620F, quad 730F

BREAKFAST
Continental (served downstairs only), 30F

30 rooms, all with bath or shower and toilet

Many hotels on Rue des Écoles are run by foreign managers for absentee owners in the Middle East. As a result, service, cleanliness, and upkeep are sometimes drastically reduced, because no one at the hotel has any stake in it, or really cares. You will find none of this at the Familia Hôtel. The Gaucherons, who have owned the hotel for almost ten years, live on site and take pride in being on top of things every minute. Theirs is a plain place, with no fancy airs, but they extend themselves so far beyond the others to accommodate their guests that the line of loyal returnees is long.

Several years ago, the bedrooms were given a much-needed overhaul. Their size didn't change, and they are still a tight fit, with limited space for bulky luggage or shopping purchases. They do, however, provide all the basics and have good mattresses, and they are neat and tidy. The bird's-eye views of Notre-Dame Cathedral are best from the front rooms on the fifth and sixth floors. Staying here puts guests only a few minutes from St-Germain-des-Prés, the islands, and all the cafés in the Latin Quarter. Métro connections are good, and so is the bus transportation.

English Spoken: Yes, and Spanish

Facilities and Services: Direct-dial phones, elevator, hair dryers, mini-bars, TVs with international reception

Nearest Tourist Attractions (Left Bank): Latin

Quarter, St-Germain-des-Prés, Île de la Cité, Île St-Louis

Grand Hôtel de Lima ★★
46, boulevard St-Germain (5th)
43 rooms, all with bath or shower and toilet

You won't find this hotel listed in many guide-books, and its fans are just as happy that it is not. So, shhh—don't tell anyone where you read about it. The legions of budget-conscious guests who have flocked here for years love it for its prime location only three minutes from Notre-Dame, and for the homey atmosphere provided by owners M. and Mme Massot—even though their refund policy is unbending.

A mirrored ground-floor entry with a long winding staircase leads to the first-floor reception desk, where a warm welcome awaits everyone. There is a beamed and paneled lounge and breakfast area next to it where you can meet fellow travelers to discuss the dos and don'ts of a visit to Paris. The bedrooms are immaculate and provide all the basics. Many have balconies, a nice bonus on a hot day in Paris. Some even have beautiful views of Notre-Dame and the Panthéon. Those on the street side are sunny but noisy. If street noise shatters your sleep, request a room on the back with no view.

English Spoken: Yes

Facilities and Services: Direct-dial phones, elevator, hair dryers, TVs in rooms with bathtubs, or to rent for 25F per night

Nearest Tourist Attractions (Left Bank): Latin Quarter, St-Michel, Notre-Dame, St-Germain-des-Prés, Panthéon, Sorbonne, Cluny Museum, Seine, Île de la Cité, Île St-Louis, shopping

TELEPHONE
46-34-02-12

TELEX
TRACE 246-918 F REF LIM 761

FAX
None

MÉTRO
Maubert-Mutualité

CREDIT CARDS
MC, B

RATES
Single 245F, double 355–455F, triple 565F, quad 655F

BREAKFAST
Continental, 35F

Grand Hôtel Oriental ★
2, rue d'Arras (5th)
32 rooms, 28 with bath or shower and toilet

There are no great surprises at the Oriental, but it is a useful Cheap Sleep in a popular Left Bank location. For the price, the rooms are amazingly clean, quiet, and recommendable. Those perches on the top

TELEPHONE
43-54-38-12

TELEX
None

FAX
(1) 40-51-86-78

MÉTRO
Cardinal-Lemoine

CREDIT CARDS
AE, MC, V

RATES
Single 122–330F, double 210–340F, triple 430F, quad 590F; hall shower 15F

BREAKFAST

floor have little balconies and views of the tips of Notre-Dame Cathedral; space in these is limited. Sure, there are chenille curtains, some marginal furniture, and a few plastic floral arrangements here and there, but for under $30 for a single, you can't expect interiors à la *Architectural Digest*. Breakfast is served in a *petit* dining room that has plastic lace tablecloths, live green plants, a cold drink machine in one corner, and a wall-mounted television set tuned into the French morning news. The desk staff tries hard, but English is limited.

English Spoken: Very limited

Facilities and Services: Direct-dial phones, elevator to 5th floor only, TV in most expensive rooms

Nearest Tourist Attractions (Left Bank): St-Michel, Rue Mouffetard, Seine, Île de la Cité, Île St-Louis

Hôtel Agora St-Germain ★★★
42, rue des Bernardins (5th)

TELEPHONE
46-34-13-00

TELEX
260-881 F

FAX
(1) 46-34-75-05

MÉTRO
Maubert-Mutualité

CREDIT CARDS
AE, DC, MC, V

RATES
Single 510–560F, double 620F, triple 760F

BREAKFAST
Continental, 45F

39 rooms, all with bath or shower and toilet

The Agora St-Germain represents a success story for both the owners and guests. It reopened in mid-1987 after undergoing a facelift of remarkable proportions and has been popular ever since for its top-quality accommodations: customized rooms with pretty silk wall coverings, ample space to move around, and smart marble and tile bathrooms. A Continental breakfast is served in a pleasing stone-walled dining room with baskets of fresh flowers and linen napkins on each table. The friendly owners, M. and Mme Lochu, and their staff see to the wishes of every guest. Now firmly recommended by all who have stayed here, this haven for weary travelers is less than five minutes away from delightful restaurants of every kind (see *Cheap Eats in Paris*) and close to all the charm and excitement of this part of the Left Bank.

English Spoken: Yes

Facilities and Services: Direct-dial phones, elevator, hair dryers, mini-bars, private room safes, radios, TVs with international reception

Nearest Tourist Attractions (Left Bank): Latin

Quarter, St-Michel, St-Germain-des-Prés, Île de la Cité, Île St-Louis

Hôtel Claude Bernard ★★★
43, rue des Écoles (5th)
30 rooms, all with bath or shower and toilet

The Claude Bernard is a mixed bag. After a 1986 remodeling project, things picked up considerably, but since then, maintenance has been spotty, and some of the pine furniture needs a dose of TLC. Aside from the constant street noise, the only other drawback for some might be the lobby with its unconventional collection of objects d'art, including a stuffed marlin over the reception desk.

Upstairs, the rooms combine English country furniture with French provincial fabrics. During the remodeling, the intricately carved moldings and doors were kept, along with the double French windows overlooking the street. The tremendous triple rooms are good family values, and the furniture can take lots more wear and tear, but they do face the noisy street, so earplugs might be a good idea for light sleepers. Despite the list of pluses and minuses, the Claude Bernard remains a Latin Quarter favorite, thanks to its friendly atmosphere and its key location as a base for exploring St-Michel, St-Germain-des-Prés, and the islands.

English Spoken: Yes

Facilities and Services: Direct-dial phones, elevator, sauna, mini-bars, TVs with international reception

Nearest Tourist Attractions (Left Bank): St-Michel, St-Germain-des-Prés, Île de la Cité, Île St-Louis, Latin Quarter

TELEPHONE
43-26-32-52

TELEX
HOTEL CB: 204-888 F

FAX
(1) 43-26-80-56

MÉTRO
Maubert-Mutualité, St-Michel

CREDIT CARDS
AE, DC, MC, V

RATES
1 or 2 persons 385-610F, triple 700F; sauna 80F

BREAKFAST
Continental, 35F

Hôtel de la Sorbonne ★★
6, rue Victor-Cousin (5th)
37 rooms, all with bath or shower and toilet

Fresh country flowers throughout and magnificent summer window boxes are the signature of owner Mme Poivier's renovated 18th-century hotel next to the Sorbonne. As you enter, you will bump into her

TELEPHONE
43-54-58-08

TELEX
206-373 F

FAX
(1) 40-51-05-18

MÉTRO
Cluny-Sorbonne, RER
Luxembourg
CREDIT CARDS
MC, V
RATES
Single 360–380F, double 360–450F, triple 500F
BREAKFAST

two dogs sleeping soundly by the reception desk. To one side is a glassed-in sitting area. Just beyond is the dining room with an incongruous display of African tribal statues mixed in with marble-topped bistro tables, black bentwood chairs, and leftover Christmas ornaments. The rooms are not luxurious or big, but they are well done in beige grass cloth, with pink bedspreads. The front lodgings are enhanced by views of the Sorbonne and Panthéon. Mme Poivier has been running her hotel for 20-plus years with a stern eye on every detail—so don't even consider loud music, room feasts, large hand laundries, or any ironing.

English Spoken: Yes

Facilities and Services: Direct-dial phones, elevator, hair dryers, TVs

Nearest Tourist Attractions (Left Bank): St-Michel, Panthéon, Sorbonne, Seine, Île de la Cité, Île St-Louis

Hôtel des Allies ★
20, rue Bertholliet (5th)
43 rooms, 10 with bath or shower and toilet

TELEPHONE
43-31-47-52
TELEX
None
FAX
(1) 45-35-13-92
MÉTRO
Censier-Daubenton
CREDIT CARDS
MC, V
RATES
Single 110–120F, double 155–265F; 30% more for extra person; hall shower 10F
BREAKFAST
Continental, 25F

Three generations of contented clientele continue to book rooms in this neat and tidy Cheap Sleep in the bottom of the fifth arrondissement. The location is not central by any means, but it is within walking distance to all the action and color around Rue Mouffetard. It is obvious money was not spent on fancy decorating touches, but all the rooms are spotless, with no rips, tears, or dents in sight, and come with price tags no Cheap Sleeper can ignore. Room No. 22 is a steal, with a huge bathroom, twin beds, and new wallpaper and paint. Number 3 on the back, with only a basin and bidet, rents for less than $40 for two, and that is a price seldom seen in any acceptable hotel in Paris today. For many, an important bonus is that credit cards are accepted. Any way you look at it, in the one-star sweepstakes, this one is a front runner.

English Spoken: Yes

Facilities and Services: None

Nearest Tourist Attractions (Left Bank): Lower end of 5th, but close to Rue Mouffetard

Hôtel des Grandes Écoles ★★
75, rue du Cardinal Lemoine (5th)
48 rooms, 39 with bath or shower and toilet

Once found, this hotel address is one that its followers whisper only to a select few. Nestled in a beautiful garden and hidden from the world behind towering wooden doors opening off the street, it is one of the most romantic havens of peace and quiet in Paris.

Two houses make up the hotel. In the one renovated in 1987 and the older one facing it, the rooms are decorated with a feminine touch, sparing no ruffle or pretty flowered fabric. Almost all of the rooms look out on the large tree-shaded garden with its trellised roses, singing birds, spring daffodils, and summer wildflowers. When you look out your window, you might well imagine you are in a French country village, not in the middle of Paris.

It is an uphill climb from the Métro, but once there you are close to the Place de la Contrescarpe, which played such an important part in Hemingway's Paris. You can also walk to Rue Mouffetard, which has a colorful daily street *marché* and some good places to eat (see *Cheap Eats in Paris*).

The grandmotherly owner, Mme Leflock, treats all her guests like members of her own family; and, of course, they wouldn't *think* of staying anyplace else. Reservations for this very special hotel are essential months in advance.

English Spoken: Yes

Facilities and Services: None in older building. In renovated building: direct-dial phones, elevator, minibars, TVs in more expensive rooms

Nearest Tourist Attractions (Left Bank): Rue Mouffetard and Place de la Contrescarpe, Panthéon, Latin Quarter

TELEPHONE
43-26-79-23

TELEX
None

FAX
(1) 43-25-28-15

MÉTRO
Cardinal Lemoine, Monge

CREDIT CARDS
MC, V

RATES
Single 260–490F, double 280–500F, triple 450F (no toilet); hall shower 15F

BREAKFAST
Continental, 30F

Hôtel des Grands Hommes ★★★
17, place du Panthéon (5th)
32 rooms, all with bath or shower and toilet

The Hôtel des Grands Hommes is one of Paris's

TELEPHONE
46-34-19-60

TELEX
PANTEOM 200-185 F

FAX
(1) 43-26-67-32

MÉTRO
St-Michel, RER Luxembourg

CREDIT CARDS
AE, DC, MC, V

RATES
Single 590F, double 700F,
triple 800F; extra bed 100F

BREAKFAST
Continental, 30F

most stylish three-star hotels, thanks to the personal management of Corinne Brethous, who is young, energetic, and full of wonderful ideas. In restoring the 18th-century building, she spared no effort to create a personal and comfortable hotel, done from top to bottom with great taste and style. The engaging bedrooms heighten the feeling that one is a guest in a lovely home, rather than in an anonymous hotel room. When reserving, request one of the front rooms with a balcony where you can have breakfast and gaze onto the Panthéon across the street and see Sacré Coeur gleaming in the distance. Honeymooners will want to stay in No. 22, with its canopied brass bed and two view balconies. The gracious formal lobby is decorated in peach colors with faux marble finishes and outfitted with plenty of soft seating, a small corner bar, and an atrium garden filled with blooming potted plants.

English Spoken: Yes

Facilities and Services: Bar, conference room, direct-dial phones, elevator, hair dryers, mini-bars, easy street parking, radios, TV with international reception

Nearest Tourist Attractions (Left Bank): Panthéon, Sorbonne, St-Michel

Hôtel des 3 Collèges ★★
16, rue Cujas (5th)

TELEPHONE
43-54-67-30

TELEX
206-034 F

FAX
(1) 46-34-02-99

MÉTRO
RER Luxembourg

CREDIT CARDS
AE, DC, MC, V

RATES
Single 325–567F, double 399–
567F, triple 735F

BREAKFAST
Continental, 40F

44 rooms, all with bath or shower and toilet

If you want a modern room with a reasonable price tag in a good Left Bank neighborhood between the Sorbonne and the Panthéon, this is the place to go. The operative word here is *simple.* The small, off-white lobby is similar to California style with its modern chairs, large green plants, and bleached wooden floors. The pocket-sized rooms have all the necessities: luggage racks, desks and chairs, full-length mirrors, wall-mounted televisions, firm mattresses, and properly fitted bathrooms. The glassed-roofed breakfast room off the lobby showcases a large green tree in the center, with white bistro tables and rattan chairs.

Management and staff are pleasant and helpful in giving directions, making dinner reservations, and confirming flights.

English Spoken: Yes

Facilities and Services: Direct-dial phones, elevator, hair dryers, TVs

Nearest Tourist Attractions (Left Bank): Panthéon, Sorbonne, St-Michel

Hôtel du Collège de France ★★
7, rue Thénard (5th)
29 rooms, all with bath or shower and toilet

Well placed in the heart of the Latin Quarter and across the street from the Collège de France, this is an outstanding value for a two-star hotel. The owner, M. Georges, is on hand every day to ensure that all runs smoothly. The pleasant rooms are uniformly done in a simple beige-and-brown color scheme. The best ones are on the top floors and have wooden beams and paneling, glimpses of Notre-Dame Cathedral, and, in summer, are equipped with portable fans. All of the rooms are immaculately clean and fully sound-proofed. The bathrooms are modern, with hair dryers, large towels, and enough space for more than just a toothbrush. The lobby and breakfast room repeat the simple color scheme, with the addition of lush green plants. The popularity of this fine little hotel is reflected in its register, which is almost completely filled months ahead, so plan accordingly.

English Spoken: Yes

Facilities and Services: Direct-dial phones, elevator to 6th floor only, TVs and radios, hair dryers, adjoining rooms, safe deposit box for 30F per week

Nearest Tourist Attractions (Left Bank): Latin Quarter, St-Michel, St-Germain-des-Prés, Sorbonne, Panthéon, Luxembourg Gardens, Seine, Île de la Cité, Île St-Louis, shopping

TELEPHONE
43-26-78-36

TELEX
None

FAX
(1) 46-34-58-29

MÉTRO
Maubert-Mutualité, St-Michel, Cluny-Sorbonne

CREDIT CARDS
AE

RATES
1 or 2 persons 480–500F; extra bed 100F

BREAKFAST
Continental, 35F in room or downstairs; if you eat downstairs, you can have all the croissants you want.

Hôtel du Panthéon ★★★
19, place du Panthéon (5th)
34 rooms, all with bath or shower and toilet

The Hôtel du Panthéon, an elegantly converted

TELEPHONE
43-54-32-95

TELEX
206-435 F

FAX
(1) 43-26-64-65

MÉTRO
Luxembourg

CREDIT CARDS
AE, DC, MC, V

RATES
Single 590F, double 700F, triple 800F

BREAKFAST
Continental, 32F

18th-century town house, faces the imposing Place du Panthéon in the fifth arrondissement. The Métro is about five blocks away, but if you love this part of Paris, you know that almost everything is within walking distance.

From the ground up, the hotel benefits from the impeccable taste and preservationist sensibilities of the gracious owner, Mme Brethous, who also owns Hôtel des Grands Hommes next door (see page 57). In this hotel she has even gone so far as to provide a shelf of reasonably current best-selling books for those guests who forgot to bring along something to read.

A dramatic entry leads to the attractive lounge with a corner coffee bar and a small atrium garden to one side. The Continental breakfast is served under the stone arches in the house's original cellar, or in the privacy of your own room. Guests will immediately feel at home in any one of the 34 rooms decorated with antique furniture, textile-covered walls, and floor-length curtains hanging from 14-foot ceilings. The front rooms facing the Panthéon are naturally in demand, but if you need absolute silence and calm, the viewless back room will guarantee this.

English Spoken: Yes

Facilities and Services: Direct-dial phones, conference room for 10, elevator, hair dryers, TVs with international reception, radios

Nearest Tourist Attractions (Left Bank): Latin Quarter, Panthéon, Luxembourg Gardens

Hôtel Esmeralda ★★
4, rue St-Julien-le-Pauvre (5th)

19 rooms, 16 with bath or shower and toilet; 4 apartments next door, all with bath or shower and toilet

TELEPHONE
43-54-19-20

TELEX
None

FAX
None

MÉTRO
St-Michel

CREDIT CARDS
None; cash only

The Esmeralda is an unconventional hideaway directly across the Seine from Notre-Dame Cathedral. It is either a hotel people love, or absolutely hate. Maybe it doesn't have the most modern accommodations in town, but it does have one of the best Left Bank locations and some of the most interesting guests. The lack of embellishments, which might disappoint some, is the lure that brings others back again and again. This is a hotel with character, for people with character.

No two rooms are alike, and, just like the charming owner, they flaunt convention and are eccentric to say the least. Some are the size of a walk-in closet; others have chandeliers, marble fireplaces, and perfect picture-postcard views of Notre-Dame over the gardens of St-Julien-le-Pauvre, Paris's oldest church. All the rooms are reached by passing through a stone-walled lobby and climbing up a winding flight of ancient stairs. Some floors slant, a few areas need a paintbrush, and others have only a nodding acquaintance with the housekeeper—and it is *noisy*. But its many cult followers don't care, because just being at the Esmeralda spells Paris for them. Bring earplugs and reserve way ahead.

Note: Insiders know to ask for one of the four apartments next door. These are, however, not for everyone. Reached via a dark, winding wooden staircase right out of Victor Hugo, the apartments offer old Paris without apologies. Yes, they are very old and dusty, and not everything works all the time. But—for some, this faded charm with a past has great appeal, especially when sitting by one of the large windows, sipping a cup of tea, and looking across the Seine to Notre-Dame.

English Spoken: Yes

Facilities and Services: Direct-dial phones for local calls only; no elevator

Nearest Tourist Attractions (Left Bank): Notre-Dame, Île de la Cité, Île St-Louis, St-Michel, St-Germain-des-Prés, Latin Quarter

Hôtel le Côlbert ★★★
7, rue de l'Hôtel Côlbert (5th)
40 rooms, all with bath or shower and toilet

I will admit it—I love Le Côlbert. For a memorable stay in Paris, you simply cannot miss at this hotel. The location is fantastic. Built around a courtyard on a tranquil, almost traffic-free street, the centuries-old town house is one minute from the Seine

RATES
Very small single 120F, 1 or 2 persons 300–450F; hall shower 15F; sauna for 2, 65F

BREAKFAST
Continental, 40F

TELEPHONE
43-25-85-65; toll free from U.S.: 800-366-1510

TELEX
260-690 F

FAX
(1) 43-25-80-19

and two from Notre-Dame. It is the perfect address for anyone who likes to wander through the winding streets around St-Michel and be within easy walking distance of many wonderful restaurants (see *Cheap Eats in Paris*).

CREDIT CARDS
AE, DC, MC, V

RATES
Single 630F, double 750–960F, suite 1,450F (3 or 4 persons), apt 1,769F (3 or 4 persons)

BREAKFAST
Continental, 50F

Polished professionalism and good old-fashioned service underscore Le Côlbert's many assets, making it one of the most sought-after small hotels in Paris. The rooms and suites are models of space and uncluttered decor, with slipper-style comfort and refined good taste. Windows in many of the rooms frame Notre-Dame Cathedral; others look over the peaked rooftops of this ancient part of Paris. In the newly redone lounge and bar, guests are invited to sip afternoon tea or to relax over cocktails in the evening.

All of this does not come at bargain prices, but as anyone who has ever stayed at Le Côlbert will tell you, it is well worth the extra francs.

English Spoken: Yes

Facilities and Services: Bar and tea salon, conference room, direct-dial phones, elevator, private room safes, TVs with international reception

Nearest Tourist Attractions (Left Bank): St-Michel, St-Germain-des-Prés, Latin Quarter, Île de la Cité, Île St-Louis, Seine, Notre-Dame

Hôtel Gay-Lussac ★
29, rue Gay-Lussac (5th)

35 rooms, none with private toilets, some with showers

TELEPHONE
43-54-23-96

TELEX
None

FAX
None

MÉTRO
Luxembourg

CREDIT CARDS
None; cash only

RATES
Single 165F, double 225–350F, triple 300–450F, quad 125F per person; hall shower 12F

BREAKFAST
Continental, 25F *included*

The sign in the reception area reads: "Don't put bottles on the windowsill. Silence of one assures rest for us all." You get the idea. This is a no-nonsense Cheap Sleep that allows no funny business.

The 35 rooms vary from not-so-bad to my-goodness-this-*is*-basic. But you are on the Left Bank, close to the Luxembourg Gardens and the RER (the suburban-transit express train) to whisk you all over Paris in a wink. The owner, and his big German shepherd named Mlle Donna, are nice; breakfast is good; and just think of all the money you will save by staying here. You can extend your Paris sojourn by at least a week, and that alone makes sleeping cheap at the Gay-Lussac worthwhile.

English Spoken: No

Facilities and Services: Direct-dial phones

Nearest Tourist Attractions (Left Bank): Luxembourg Gardens, Panthéon, Latin Quarter

Le Jardin de Cluny ★★★
9, rue du Sommerard (5th)

40 rooms, all with bath or shower and toilet

Refined comfort and Parisian elegance are the hallmarks of the redecorated Jardin de Cluny. Occupying a pivotal Left Bank location between Boulevard St-Michel and Boulevard St-Germain, it is close to all the fun, glamor, and bright lights this animated *quartier* has to offer.

The uniformly designed rooms have black wicker furnishings and a soothing Oriental theme. I like No. 601, a combination bedroom and sitting room with huge closets and a view of the spires of Notre-Dame, or the large top-floor family suite that boasts a view of the Cathedral from the bathroom.

Breakfast is served on Villeroy and Bosch china in a stone-walled dining room. Nicely upholstered chairs arranged around large tables make this a pleasant place to start the day with a Continental breakfast or just a glass of orange juice.

English Spoken: Yes

Facilities and Services: Bar, direct-dial phones, elevator, hair dryers, mini-bars, TVs with international reception

Nearest Tourist Attractions (Left Bank): Latin Quarter, St-Germain-des-Prés, Cluny Museum, Île de la Cité, Île St-Louis

TELEPHONE
43-54-22-66; toll free from U.S. and Canada: 800-528-1234

TELEX
206-295 F

FAX
(1) 40-51-03-36

MÉTRO
Maubert-Mutualité

CREDIT CARDS
AE, DC, MC, V

RATES
Single 504–526F, double 565–690F, triple 675F, suite 910F

BREAKFAST
Continental, included; cannot be deducted

Hôtel Marignan ★
13, rue du Sommerard (5th)

30 rooms, none with bath or shower and toilet. All facilities are in the hall, and showers are free

The Marignan lives up to the four C's of all Cheap Sleepers: it is Clean, Convenient, Comfortable, and Cheap, especially in November and December when

TELEPHONE
43-54-63-81

TELEX
None

FAX
None

MÉTRO
Maubert-Mutualité
CREDIT CARDS
None; cash only
RATES
Single 145F, double 230–260F,
triple 295–395F; hall shower
free
BREAKFAST
Continental, included; cannot
be deducted

rooms for two, three, or four people are 15 percent less than the published prices. The hotel is usually jammed year round with a frugal crowd of students, backpackers, and professors. A spirit of camaraderie prevails in this busy spot, making it impossible to feel lonely for long. The friendly management has for more than 35 years provided guests with a wealth of information on Paris, including a large detailed map of the *quartier* showing the Métros, banks, pharmacies, money exchange offices, bakeries, and tourist sites. The management also clearly sets the rules of the hotel, and guests are expected to abide by them or move out. Don't worry, the rules aren't that bad—just sensible guides to guarantee the comfort of each guest.

English Spoken: Yes

Facilities and Services: Basement laundry and ironing area (no room laundry allowed); dining area where guests can eat food brought in

Nearest Tourist Attractions (Left Bank): Cluny Museum, Latin Quarter, St-Michel, St-Germain-des-Prés, Île de la Cité, Île St-Louis

Le Jardin des Plantes ★★
5, rue Linné (5th)

TELEPHONE
47-07-06-20
TELEX
PLANTEL 203-684 F
FAX
(1) 47-07-62-74
MÉTRO
Jussieu
CREDIT CARDS
AE, DC, MC, V
RATES
Single 340–580F, double 400–
620F; extra bed 100F; sauna
65F (1 hour)
BREAKFAST
Continental, 40F

33 rooms, all with bath or shower and toilet

Le Jardin des Plantes, beautifully situated across from the Botanical Gardens, is one of my favorite Left Bank hotels, and anyone who has ever stayed here feels the same way. The French would call it *mignon*, which means pretty and graceful. Gault-Millau terms it "irresistible." It is all of these things and more: a very comfortable two-star hotel with many features not often found in a four-star.

Owner Françoise Bompard has spared no effort to pamper and please her guests. All 33 rooms are decorated in an individual floral theme with one flower predominating. If you are in the iris room, everything will be coordinated in an iris theme, from the curtains and bedspreads to the tile in the bathroom and the breakfast tray carrying your hot chocolate and croissants. Creature comforts have not been overlooked in the scheme of things: double-paned windows buffer street noise; blackout drapes allow for late mornings; the sauna in the basement helps to ease sightseeing aches; and an iron and ironing board are available if your clothes have developed that "lived-in" look. Information sheets give specific directions by Métro, bus, and foot to tourist must-dos in Paris, and stationery is available so you can write to your friends at home to rave about your Parisian vacation. Breakfast is served either in the rooms, on a flower-decked fifth-floor view garden, or in a downstairs room that becomes a restaurant for lunch and a delightful tearoom in the late afternoon. In the stone cellar lounge, local artists display their works on a monthly changing basis.

English Spoken: Yes

Facilities and Services: Bar, direct-dial phones, elevator, hair dryers, mini-bars, TVs with international reception, iron and ironing board, restaurant and room service, sauna, monthly art exhibits

Nearest Tourist Attractions (Left Bank): Botanical Gardens, Latin Quarter, Île de la Cité, Île St-Louis, St-Germain-des-Prés, Rue Mouffetard

Le Notre Dame Hôtel ★★★
1, quai St-Michel (5th)
26 rooms, all with bath or shower and toilet

Refashioned with verve a few years ago, this excellent hotel offers 26 beautiful rooms to lovers of Notre-Dame's architectural beauty. Ask for a room facing the street, and you will be able to look out across the booksellers lining the *quais* along the Seine and onto the great western facade of Notre-Dame Cathedral. You will go to sleep and wake with the sights and sounds of Paris, but the majestic view will be worth it.

Entrance to the hotel is through a mirrored ground-floor hall and up a short flight of steps. The inviting sitting room off the reception area has picture windows facing the cathedral, and is a relaxing place to be on a cool day, sitting by the open fire, sipping a drink, and watching *toute* Paris surge by. The rooms display a smart mix of antiques and reproductions and are comfortable, if small. My favorite is No. 22, a

TELEPHONE
43-54-20-43

TELEX
206-650 F

FAX
(1) 43-26-61-75

MÉTRO
St-Michel

CREDIT CARDS
AE, DC, MC, V

RATES
1 or 2 persons 570–770F, suite or duplex 1,050F

BREAKFAST
Continental, 40F

corner room with two windows overlooking Notre-Dame. Another nice room is the suite, but for some, the steep ladder stairs to the sitting area could be difficult to maneuver. Management overlooks nothing, and quality service is provided to each guest. Tabs are rather high, but not when you consider the sublime location.

English Spoken: Yes

Facilities and Services: Bar, direct-dial phones, elevator, hair dryers, mini-bars, TVs; street parking almost impossible, must use a parking garage

Nearest Tourist Attractions (Left Bank): Notre-Dame, Île de la Cité, Île St-Louis, Seine, St-Michel, St-Germain-des-Prés

Hôtel Parc Saint-Séverin ★★★
22, rue de la Parcheminerie (5th)

27 rooms, all with bath or shower and toilet

TELEPHONE
43-54-32-17

TELEX
270-950 F OSEVRIN

FAX
(1) 43-54-70-71

MÉTRO
St-Michel

CREDIT CARDS
AE, MC, V

RATES
Single 500–900F, double 600–900F, extra-large room with sitting area 950F, penthouse 1,350F

BREAKFAST
Continental, 50F

Dyed-in-the-wool aficionados of life around St-Michel, who also like elegantly understated surroundings, will love this hotel. The owners are to be applauded for turning a rundown building into an alluring, modern establishment that is serene, serious, and pleasing to the eye. Instead of large bouquets in the lobby and reception area, there might be one perfect branch of orchids displayed against a cool gray wall, or two abstract paintings complementing the breakfast room. For someone very, very special, reserve No. 70, the private penthouse suite with its own elevator entrance. The wraparound terrace provides unequalled views of Notre-Dame, St-Séverin Church (which is one of the most popular in Paris for weddings), the Panthéon, Collège de France, Tour Montparnasse, and, in the distance, the Eiffel Tower, and Sacré Coeur on Montmartre. The interior of this dream suite glows with a blend of antiques and contemporary furnishings. The other rooms in the hotel maintain the same standards of excellence, and many have impressive views. For those who want up-to-the-minute convenience and luxury in the heart of ancient Paris, the Parc Saint-Séverin is justifiably higher priced.

English Spoken: Yes

Facilities and Services: Direct-dial phones, elevator, mini-bars, TVs, some rooms with private safes

Nearest Tourist Attractions (Left Bank): St-Michel, Cluny Museum, St-Germain-des-Prés, Île de la Cité, Île St-Louis, Latin Quarter

Select Hôtel ★★★
1, place de la Sorbonne (5th)
69 rooms, all with bath or shower and toilet

In 1937 Eric Sevareid paid 50¢ a night at the Select. Things have changed—considerably.

Dramatically renovated in late 1987, the hotel now has one of the most spectacular interior garden courts in Paris, complete with blooming tropical plants, a waterfall, and singing birds. The lobby is a study in ultramodern decor, with chrome and black leather furniture highlighted by posters of Paris. This sleek approach is carried into the intimate bar and breakfast room.

The rooms have as much appeal as the public areas, especially those overlooking the garden court or the interesting Place de la Sorbonne in front. All the rooms skillfully combine the best of the old with the practicality and convenience of the new. One of the nicest is No. 33, which displays the original stone wall of the hotel and centuries-old oak beams. Two large floor-to-ceiling windows open onto the *place* below. Comfortable armchairs, good reading lights, a large working desk, hidden storage space, and a nice bath make this a favorite for longer stays.

A friendly, outgoing desk staff, an ideal Latin Quarter location, and all the creature comforts make this hotel a front runner in the *quartier*. Unfortunately, it will cost more than 50¢ a night.

English Spoken: Yes

Facilities and Services: Air-conditioning in some rooms, bar with light snacks, conference room, direct-dial phones, hair dryers, elevator, TVs, radios

Nearest Tourist Attractions (Left Bank): Latin Quarter, St-Germain-des-Prés, Île de la Cité, Île St-Louis, Sorbonne

TELEPHONE
46-34-14-80

TELEX
201-207 F

FAX
(1) 46-34-51-79

MÉTRO
St-Michel, Luxembourg

CREDIT CARDS
AE, DC, MC, V

RATES
Single 530–590F, double 590–690F, triple 860F, apartment 1,040F

BREAKFAST
Continental if served in room, buffet served downstairs; included and cannot be deducted

SIXTH ARRONDISSEMENT

SIXTH ARRONDISSEMENT
Left Bank: École des Beaux-Arts, Luxembourg Gardens, Odéon National Theater, St-Germain-des-Prés Church, St-Sulpice Church

This area is a continuation of the Latin Quarter and one of the most stimulating parts of the city. Intellectual, elegant, and artistic, it has tiny side streets, old buildings, antiques shops, a thriving café life, and more atmosphere block for block than anyone could ever soak up. The Square by the St-Germain Church, the oldest in Paris, is the main focus of the district. Aux Deux Magots and Café de Flore, the two most celebrated cafés in Paris, were the hangouts of Hemingway, Sartre, Simone de Beauvoir, and James Joyce. Today they are jammed with Parisians and tourists alike engaged in premier people-watching.

HOTELS IN THE SIXTH ARRONDISSEMENT

Crystal Hôtel ★★
Grand Hôtel des Balcons ★★
Hôtel Aviatic ★★★
Hôtel Danemark ★★★
Hôtel d'Angleterre ★★★
Hôtel de Buci ★
Hôtel de Fleurie ★★★
Hôtel l'Abbaye Saint-Germain ★★★
Hôtel de l'Odéon ★★★
Hôtel des Académies ★
Hôtel des Deux Continents ★★
Hôtel du Lys ★
Hôtel Eugénie ★★
Hôtel Ferrandi ★★★
Hôtel le Saint-Grégoire ★★★
Hôtel Louis II ★★★
Hôtel Saint-André-des-Arts ★
Hôtel Saint-Germain-des-Prés ★★★
Hôtel Saint-Michel ★
Hôtel Saint-Paul ★★★
Hôtel Saint-Pierre ★★
L'Atelier Montparnasse Hôtel ★★★
Latitudes ★★★
Left Bank Hôtel ★★★
Odéon Hôtel ★★★
Pension de Famille Poirier **no stars**
Pension les Marronniers **no stars**

Regent's Hôtel ★★
Villa des Artistes ★★★
Welcome Hôtel ★★

Crystal Hôtel ★★
24, rue St-Benoît (6th)

26 rooms, all with bath or shower and toilet

For a prime Left Bank position within walking distance to all St-Germain has to offer, from café sitting and watching street mimes to indulging in great shopping, reserve a room at the Crystal Hôtel. Run with dedication and care by Mme Choukroun, there has been a long list of happy guests over years, from James Thurber and his wife Helen to today's actors, writers, and producers on their way up. All the rooms are different and are furnished mostly in 19th-century English style with tiny-flowered wallpaper and matching curtains, or are painted a soft pastel with a coordinating spread. Some have beams, others a skylight with afternoon sun. From a few, guests can see the lighted St-Germain-des-Prés church at night. Reservations are hard to come by during peak periods, so make yours as early as possible.

English Spoken: Yes

Facilities and Services: Direct-dial phones, elevator to all but top floor, room safes, TVs

Nearest Tourist Attractions (Left Bank): St-Germain, Île de la Cité, Seine

TELEPHONE
45-48-85-14

TELEX
201-021 F

FAX
(1) 45-49-16-45

MÉTRO
St-Germain-des-Prés

CREDIT CARDS
AE, DC, MC, V

RATES
Single 485–630F, double 485–735F, triple 850F, suite 1,050F

BREAKFAST
Continental, 45F extra

Grand Hôtel des Balcons ★★ ∨
3, rue Casimir-Delavigne (6th)

55 rooms, all with bath or shower and toilet

The Grand Hôtel des Balcons is one of the most dignified low-budget hotels in this part of the Left Bank, and a perennial favorite with older, cost-conscious budgeteers.

The huge lobby is a masterpiece of Art Nouveau design, with glorious stained-glass windows and masterfully turned wood. There are always beautiful fresh flower displays, arranged by the manager's wife, who is a recognized ikebana expert. Some of the rooms are

TELEPHONE
46-34-78-50

TELEX
None

FAX
(1) 46-34-06-27

MÉTRO
Odéon

CREDIT CARDS
MC, V

RATES
1 or 2 persons 300–400F,
triple 475F
BREAKFAST
Continental, 40F

beginning to unravel around the edges, not everything even begins to match, and the baths tend to be small and vintage. On the up side, most rooms have nice wallpaper, good reading lights, and little balconies with views. The uniformed maids keep thing ship-shape, and the non-smiling management keeps an eagle eye out for room picnics and dripping laundry. The location is top drawer, close to loads of budget restaurants (see *Cheap Eats in Paris*) and near Place de l'Odéon, Boulevard St-Michel, St-Germain-des-Prés, and one of the city's most wonderful and famed parks, the Luxembourg Gardens.

English Spoken: Yes

Facilities and Services: Direct-dial phones, elevator, TVs, radios

Nearest Tourist Attractions (Left Bank): St-Germain-des-Prés, St-Michel, Luxembourg Gardens, Île de la Cité, Île St-Louis

Hôtel Aviatic ★★★
105, rue de Vaugirard (6th)

TELEPHONE
45-44-38-21
TELEX
200-372 F
FAX
(1) 45-49-35-83
MÉTRO
St-Placide, Montparnasse
CREDIT CARDS
AE, DC, MC, V
RATES
Single 610F, double 680F,
triple 820F, 2 parking spaces
75F per night
BREAKFAST
Continental, included; cannot
be deducted

43 rooms, all with bath or shower and toilet

The Art Deco glass and black wrought-iron awning over the door flanked by two brass and copper lamps sets the welcoming stage for this warm and inviting family-run hotel. The gracious lobby has faux marble columns and intimate groupings of velvet chairs and antique marble chests topped with bouquets of fresh flowers. To one side is a comfortable breakfast room papered with vintage Parisian art posters. A wide, winding stairway with overhead skylights leads guests up to forest green carpeted hallways to the 43 redone rooms in two buildings. There is more than just a touch of class in these well-thought-out chambers, which all have built-in luggage racks, good spreading-out space, armchair seating, and huge closets. The rooms in the front building are bright and airy, with pretty views of the surrounding Montparnasse neighborhood. Those in the back are sunny, but there isn't much of a view.

English Spoken: Yes

Facilities and Services: Direct-dial phones, eleva-

tor, some hair dryers, mini-bars, 2 parking spaces, TVs

Nearest Tourist Attractions (Left Bank): Montparnasse

Hôtel Danemark ★★★
21, rue Vavin (6th)
15 rooms, all with bath or shower and toilet

For the Nurit family, nothing seems to be too much trouble in pleasing their guests. They have a special fondness for Americans, many of whom have been repeat guests for years, even before the hotel was what it is today. The Nurits are proud of their 15-room hotel in Montparnasse, and they should be. It is an imaginative lesson in how to take an old student-style hotel and turn it into an eye-catching spot on the cutting edge of hotel chic.

Cool blues and grays dominate the color scheme, with artist-inspired furnishings that look like exhibits from the Museum of Modern Art in New York. The walls are dotted with an interesting collection of dramatic posters of Parisian landmarks and famous race cars. The rooms are small and compact, but provide everything for a comfortable stay. Each has its own Italian marble bathroom with heated towel racks, an overhead fan, and, in a few, a Jacuzzi.

English Spoken: Yes

Facilities and Services: Bar, direct-dial phones, elevator, hair dryers, Jacuzzis in a few rooms, mini-bars, TVs

Nearest Tourist Attractions (Left Bank): Montparnasse

TELEPHONE
43-26-93-78

TELEX
202-568 F

FAX
(1) 46-34-66-06

MÉTRO
Vavin, Notre-Dame-des-Champs

CREDIT CARDS
AE, DC, MC, V

RATES
1 or 1 persons 590F; Jacuzzi in room 100F extra

BREAKFAST
Continental, 40F

Hôtel d'Angleterre ★★★
44, rue Jacob (6th)
25 rooms, all with bath or shower and toilet

Benjamin Franklin refused to enter this building to sign the Treaty of Paris because it was the British Embassy and considered British soil. Ernest Hemingway had no qualms about it when he occupied room No. 14, describing it to his friends as "good and cheap."

TELEPHONE
42-60-34-72

TELEX
None

FAX
(1) 42-60-16-93

MÉTRO
St-Germain-des-Prés

CREDIT CARDS
AE, DC, MC, V
RATES
1 or 2 persons 750–900F
(standard room), 950–1,050F
(deluxe room or suite); extra
bed, add 30 percent
BREAKFAST
Continental, 49F

Today the Angleterre is no longer "cheap," but a declared national monument and a well-known classic hotel with a long list of guests clamoring to get in. Its only flaw continues to be the very frosty desk staff, which probably will be replaced when management receives enough letters of complaint.

The traditional rooms and suites are all different but perfectly executed, with high ceilings, exposed beams, large beds, exceptional closet space, and fabulous double-sink bathrooms. The lobby offers a bar and an intimate piano lounge. Breakfast is served in a sunny dining room with well-spaced comfortable seating and good lighting for reading the morning papers. The rates are on the high side, but the hotel is included for those seeking a distinguished location in one of the most popular tourist *quartiers* in Paris. When reserving, be sure to specify either a standard room or a deluxe room or suite, and get a written confirmation from the hotel. While all the accommodations are lovely, the standard rooms might be rather small for two people with bulky luggage.

English Spoken: Yes

Facilities and Services: Bar, direct-dial phones, elevator in main building, TVs

Nearest Tourist Attractions (Left Bank): Superb shopping and browsing, St-Germain-des-Prés, St-Michel, Île de la Cité, Île St-Louis

Hôtel de Buci ★
22, rue de Buci (6th)

TELEPHONE
43-26-89-22
TELEX
None
FAX
(1) 46-33-80-31
MÉTRO
St-Germain-des-Prés,
Mabillon, Odéon
CREDIT CARDS
MC, V
RATES
Single 200–310F, double 360–
450F, triple 450F; hall shower
20F

25 rooms, 20 with bath or shower and toilet

Devoted regulars swear by this one-star gem for several reasons. To begin with, it has reasonable rates for the area and photogenic views of a bustling Parisian street life that runs on a 24-hour schedule. While the rooms will appear faded to some, they do have a certain artsy Left Bank charm, thanks to the antique brass beds, the Tiffany ceiling lights, and the old armoires placed throughout. Finally, this is the area where Jean-Paul Sartre lived, where Hemingway wrote and drank, and bohemians of all ages and nationalities gather today. For the ultimate in Parisian atmosphere, you cannot beat it. It can be extremely noisy, especially on weekends and holidays, so if this is a problem for you, don't forget the earplugs.

English Spoken: Some

Facilities and Services: Direct-dial phones, no elevator

Nearest Tourist Attractions (Left Bank): St-Germain-des-Prés, St-Michel, Île de la Cité, Île St-Louis, Seine

Hôtel de Fleurie ★★★
32-34, rue Grégoire-de-Tours (6th)
29 rooms, all with bath or shower and toilet

If you enjoy the color, animation, noise, and round-the-clock atmosphere of St-Germain-des-Prés, then the Hôtel de Fleurie is for you. This exceptional hotel is owned and managed by the Marolleau family, who for two generations owned Brasserie Balzar (see *Cheap Eats in Paris*). When they sold the brasserie a few years ago, they bought this hotel and, through a labor of love and a year of hard work, completely transformed it.

The facade of the hotel has been restored to its former glory and embellished with statues that are lighted at night. The inside is no less inspiring. The lobby and salon are models of gracious comfort and charm, showcasing Mme Marolleau's stunning collection of Art Nouveau plant and flower containers. A spiral staircase leads from the reception desk down to a stone-walled breakfast room where fresh orange juice, cheese, and homemade breakfast cakes are included in the Continental breakfast. Almost all of the rooms have a spacious modern bath and a good layout of space. All rooms are equipped with a mini-bar, a remote-controlled television, and fluffy white terry robes for after showering. Room No. 60, on the top floor with no elevator access, overlooks a beautiful mosaic-tiled building across the street. This room is big enough for long stays and has the added benefit of air-conditioning during the dog days of Parisian summers.

English Spoken: Yes

BREAKFAST
Continental, included; cannot be deducted

TELEPHONE
43-29-59-81

TELEX
206-153 F

FAX
(1) 43-29-68-44

MÉTRO
Odéon

CREDIT CARDS
AE, DC, MC, V

RATES
Single 550F, double 700F, deluxe rooms 950F; extra bed 150F

BREAKFAST
Continental (with cheese, juice, and pastries), 45F

Facilities and Services: Bar, direct-dial phones, elevator to all but top floor, hair dryers, mini-bars, private room safes, TVs with international reception

Nearest Tourist Attractions (Left Bank): St-Germain-des-Prés, St-Michel, Île de la Cité, Île St-Louis

Hôtel de l'Abbaye Saint-Germain ★★★
10, rue Cassette (6th)

44 rooms, all with bath or shower and toilet

TELEPHONE
45-44-38-11

TELEX
None

FAX
(1) 45-48-07-86

MÉTRO
St-Sulpice

CREDIT CARDS
V

RATES
Standard room 800F (1 or 2 persons), larger double 1,250F, suite 1,800F

BREAKFAST
Continental, included; cannot be deducted

In the 16th and 17th centuries, the Abbaye Saint-Germain was a Catholic convent. Today it is the favorite hotel of many who love its quiet location, discreet staff, and commendable service. The entrance is off the street through 15-foot-high green doors that open onto a plant-filled cobblestoned courtyard where the nuns once gathered before going to chapel for daily prayers. The central reception room is handsomely furnished with magnificent antiques and comfortable sofas centered around a marble fireplace. Behind this is an exquisite garden salon with intimate seating, a profusion of flowers, and a nice bar. Returnees especially like the top-floor suites, with their arched ceilings and rooftop views, and the two ground-floor rooms with a private garden.

Because the Abbaye Saint-Germain is so special, it is higher in price and is included for those whose budgets allow for more flexibility.

English Spoken: Yes

Facilities and Services: Bar, direct-dial phones, elevator, some hair dryers, TVs with international reception in larger rooms and suites, light meals, room service

Nearest Tourist Attractions (Left Bank): Latin Quarter, Luxembourg Gardens, St-Germain-des-Prés, St-Sulpice, good shopping

Hôtel de l'Odéon ★★★
13, rue St-Sulpice (6th)

TELEPHONE
43-25-70-11

TELEX
206-731 F

29 rooms, all with bath or shower and toilet

Hôtel de l'Odéon has become a popular Paris destination for travelers who want luxury and impeccable service in a distinguished hotel that is still small enough to maintain a personal touch.

The interior is in the style of a 17th-century inn, beautifully blending antique charm and atmosphere with all the modern conveniences one expects in a three-star hotel. In the charm department, the Odéon has everything: high beamed ceilings, stunning furniture, massive tapestries, intricately scrolled brass and metal beds with hand-crocheted coverlets, skylights, blooming flower boxes under the windows, and lovely oils and watercolors throughout. Recent improvements include a remodeled back building and the addition of a manicured garden. On the convenience side, the baths are large, the bedside lighting good, double-paned windows keep street noise to a minimum, and the closets are large enough for more than the contents of an overnight bag.

English Spoken: Yes

Facilities and Services: Air-conditioning in 10 rooms, bar, direct-dial phones, elevator to all floors in main building and to 4th in back, hair dryers, room safes, radios, TVs with international reception

Nearest Tourist Attractions (Left Bank): St-Germain-des-Prés, Latin Quarter, St-Sulpice, St-Michel, Île de la Cité, Île St-Louis, Luxembourg Gardens

FAX
(1) 43-29-97-34

MÉTRO
Odéon

CREDIT CARDS
AE, DC, MC, V

RATES
Single 590–750F, double 780–800F, triple 900F

BREAKFAST
Continental, 40F

Hôtel des Académies ★
15, rue de la Grande Chaumiére (6th)
21 rooms, 17 with bath or shower and toilet

When planning your trip to Paris, you may wonder where all the non-millionaires sleep. Many of them have slept at Hôtel des Académies, where you won't have to dig too deeply into your pockets to pay your final bill. The owner, Mme Charles, was born in the hotel almost 80 years ago and still lives there, running it with a firm hand, not standing for even a hint of hanky-panky. Her plain little upstairs Montparnasse location delivers small but spotless rooms at unheard-of rates. There are no extras, and the rooms mix 1950s chrome and plastic with semi-antiques and varying color schemes. But with those

TELEPHONE
43-26-66-44

TELEX
None

FAX
None

MÉTRO
Vavin

CREDIT CARDS
None; cash only

RATES
Single 125F (small, for students), double 175–230F; hall shower 10F

BREAKFAST
Continental (no croissants), 22F; served in room only

breathtakingly low prices, who cares? Certainly not the generations of families who return year after year, making it their home base in Paris.

English Spoken: None
Facilities and Services: None
Nearest Tourist Attractions (Left Bank): Montparnasse, Luxembourg Gardens

Hôtel des Deux Continents ★★
25, rue Jacob (6th)

TELEPHONE
43-26-72-46

TELEX
None

FAX
None

MÉTRO
St-Germain-des-Prés

CREDIT CARDS
MC, V

RATES
Single 380–550F, double 450–575F, triple 625F

BREAKFAST
Continental, 35F

40 rooms, all with bath or shower and toilet

Deux Continents has an enviable Left Bank location surrounded by avant-garde art galleries and shops where you can browse among Art Deco wonders, hand-painted tarot cards, amusing antiques, and fabulous period furniture. The hotel is a stone's throw away from Boulevard St-Germain and its famous cafés, and around the corner from Place Furstenburg and the atelier where Delacroix painted.

The concern and dedication of the charming owner, Mme Chresteil, and her long-time manager, M. Gilles Rouaulat, is apparent, from the rest of the friendly staff to the uniformed maids who diligently uphold Madame's high standards. The hotel is made up of three separate houses connected by a honeycomb of corridors, staircases, flower-filled courtyards, and walkways. If stairs are a problem, request a room in the first house. Here the rooms are generally larger, and there is an elevator. All the rooms, cozily furnished in a mix of the modern and the not-so-modern, are light, bright, airy and spotlessly clean, with ample wardrobes, full mirrors, and good reading lights. All in all, this is a solid value in an intriguing part of Paris.

English Spoken: Yes
Facilities and Services: Direct-dial phones, elevator in 1st house only, TVs with international reception
Nearest Tourist Attractions (Left Bank): Latin Quarter, St-Germain-des-Prés, St-Sulpice, St-Michel, Seine, Île de la Cité, Île St-Louis

Hôtel du Lys ★
23, rue Serpente (6th)
21 rooms, 18 with bath or shower and toilet

When I first walked into the Hôtel du Lys, I could not believe it had only one star—it has more charm and romantic appeal than many three-stars in the area that charge twice as much. The owner, Marie-Hélèn-Steffen, who took over when her father retired after running the hotel for 50 years, told me that she preferred to operate the hotel as a one-star rather than deal with all the red tape and extra taxes that adding one or more stars would cause. The bottom line for guests is great: you get more for your money, and in this day and age, that is always a welcome surprise.

Of course there is no elevator, the air-conditioning consists of opening the window, and there are no TV sets or videos to amuse you. But who needs all that? This is Paris, in the heart of the wonderful Left Bank, and your time should be spent exploring, not lounging in a hotel room.

The rooms are all exceptionally nice. They are done in a cozy *vielle* French style with beams, a stone wall here and there, and matching chintz spreads and curtains. Even the exposed plumbing pipes are painted to match the room's color scheme. Although a few rooms have no toilets, all have a shower and are very clean. All in all, this is a Cheap Sleep high on the A list.

English Spoken: Sometimes

Facilities and Services: Direct-dial phones, hair dryers

Nearest Tourist Attractions (Left Bank): St-Michel, St-Germain-des-Prés, Île de la Cité, Île St-Louis, Latin Quarter

TELEPHONE
43-26-97-57

TELEX
None

FAX
None

MÉTRO
St-Michel, Odéon

CREDIT CARDS
None; cash only

RATES
Single 300F, double 400F, triple 450F

BREAKFAST
Continental, included; cannot be deducted

Hôtel Eugénie ★★
31, rue St-André-des-Arts (6th)
30 rooms, all with bath or shower and toilet

Situated on one of the most animated pedestrian streets in the very core of old Paris, the Eugénie offers good value for your hotel franc, and gives you pulsat-

TELEPHONE
43-26-29-03

TELEX
201-438 F

FAX
(1) 43-29-75-60

MÉTRO
St-Michel, Odéon

CREDIT CARDS
AE, DC, MC, V

RATES
Single 385–450F, double 485–
580F; extra bed, add 30%

BREAKFAST
Continental, 40F

ing, round-the-clock atmosphere in the bargain. The upbeat little rooms in blues, greens, and pinks have double-paned windows, remote-controlled TVs, and are big enough to turn around in. They are, however, short on luggage and closet space. The baths have the extras that tend to make a difference: hair dryers, nice towels, and the latest fixtures. The staff is diligent, and helpful with directions and tips about the area.

English Spoken: Yes

Facilities and Services: Direct-dial phones, elevator, hair dryers, mini-bars, mini-safes in rooms (20F per day), TVs with international reception

Nearest Tourist Attractions (Left Bank): St-Germain-des-Prés, Île de la Cité, Île St-Louis, St-Michel, shopping

Hôtel Ferrandi ★★★
92, rue du Cherche-Midi (6th)
42 rooms, all with bath or shower and toilet

TELEPHONE
42-22-97-40

TELEX
205-210 F

FAX
(1) 45-44-89-97

MÉTRO
Sèvres-Babylone

CREDIT CARDS
AE, DC, MC, V

RATES
Single 400F, double 520–
880F; suite 1,200F; parking
75F per night (must reserve
space when reserving room)

BREAKFAST
Continental, 50F

Once one of the best-kept secrets in Paris, the Ferrandi is now on everyone's top-ten list of wonderful small hotels. Thoroughly dignified in every way, the hotel displays an unusually successful combination of the best in old-world style and service with modern comforts and expectations. The attractive owner, Mme La Fond, is on hand every day to stay on top of details that make the difference in a guest's stay.

The hallways, lined with ocher fabric, are gracefully joined by a winding staircase painted in faux marble. The beautiful rooms are furnished with period antiques, are coordinated in soft shades of blues, browns, and pinks, and have all the comforts of home. Most have extra closet and luggage space and are just the ticket for those of us who don't travel lightly. For longer stays, I like room No. 50, a two-room apartment with a large marble bath. Some of the bathrooms, especially in the smaller rooms, tend to be cramped, but most are equipped with heated towel racks, and all have an assortment of soaps and toiletries. Motorists will appreciate the hotel garage, and shoppers will love all the discount shopping stores within easy reach.

English Spoken: Yes

Facilities and Services: Bar, direct-dial phones, mini-bars in some rooms, TVs and radios, private parking

Nearest Tourist Attractions (Left Bank): Montparnasse, Luxembourg Gardens, Bon Marché department store (all quite a walk); good discount shopping (close)

Hôtel le Saint-Grégoire ★★★
43, rue de l'Abbé Grégoire (6th)
20 rooms, all with bath or shower and toilet

TELEPHONE
45-48-23-23

TELEX
205-343 F

FAX
(1) 45-58-33-95

MÉTRO
St-Placide, Rennes

CREDIT CARDS
AE, DC, MC, V

RATES
1 or 2 persons 650–800F, suites 1,120F

BREAKFAST
Continental (with juice and yogurt), 55F

Everyone is talking about it because on all counts the Hôtel le Saint-Grégoire is a winner. Although it is on the high side for a Cheap Sleep, I can assure you it is worth every *sou*, not only for the comfort and surroundings, but for the welcome and assistance extended by the staff, skillfully headed by M. François de Béné.

The color scheme is purple, yellow, orange, red, and beige—and it works. Decorator David Hicks has created an elegantly intimate atmosphere in this 20-room hotel by mixing period antiques with handsome modern pieces and sprinkling interesting fabrics and rich silks throughout a garden setting. As a result, the entire hotel has a rich feeling of well-being, from the fireplace in the rose-filled lobby to the linen-clad tables in the *cave* dining room, where orange juice and yogurt are served with the Continental breakfast.

Please forward all mail to me care of room No. 100, a bright yellow fantasy with a marble-topped coffee table, a bureau large enough to hold my belongings, and two comfortable chairs for lazy late-night reading. The bathroom has heated towel racks and enough fluffy towels to last almost forever. After one or two nights at this hotel, you will wish you never had to leave Paris.

English Spoken: Yes

Facilities and Services: Bar, direct-dial phones, elevator, hair dryers, TVs, some air-conditioned rooms, room service from La Marlotte Restaurant (owned by hotel; see *Cheap Eats in Paris*)

Nearest Tourist Attractions (Left Bank): Luxembourg Gardens, discount shopping

Hôtel Louis II ★★★
2, rue St-Sulpice (6th)

22 rooms, all with bath or shower and toilet

TELEPHONE
46-33-13-80

TELEX
206-561 F

FAX
(1) 46-33-17-29

MÉTRO
Odéon

CREDIT CARDS
AE, DC, MC, V

RATES
1 or 2 persons 500–650F,
triple 800F

BREAKFAST
Continental, 38F (served
anytime); includes yogurt,
fruit, and juice

Restored in the style of Louis II, with beams, brocade, red-tiled floors, and graceful, hand-rubbed antiques, this hotel is one of the best examples of what a little imagination, taste, and money can do to revive an exhausted Left Bank site. All the old wood alcoves and rooms under the eaves were saved. Flowered wallpaper, lacy bed covers, and period furnishings were combined to create the homey bedchambers. An elegant salon off the main entrance has facilities for serving morning coffee and afternoon tea, and manager Brigitte Siozade works overtime to satisfy the needs of her many returning guests. It would be all just perfect if the rooms were a bit bigger and the bathrooms more functional, if any luggage space existed, and if the closets held more. If you are traveling alone or only with hand luggage, however, and you love the charm of this part of romantic Paris, then this hotel is a strong contender.

English Spoken: Yes

Facilities and Services: Direct-dial phones, elevator, hair dryer, mini-bars, room safes, TVs and radios

Nearest Tourist Attractions (Left Bank): St-Germain-des-Prés, Luxembourg Gardens, St-Michel, Île de la Cité, Île St-Louis, shopping

Hôtel Saint-André-des-Arts ★
66, rue St-André-des-Arts (6th)

34 rooms, 25 with bath or shower and toilet

TELEPHONE
43-26-96-16

TELEX
None

FAX
None

MÉTRO
Odéon

CREDIT CARDS
None; cash only

Warning: This hotel is not for everyone. The location is strategic; the prices are low; and the nonconventional crowd of fashion groupies, hip musicians, budding actors, and starving backpackers is party-loving and carefree. For some, the rooms are so small that cabin fever sets in immediately. Others may object to the unpleasant symphony of noises drifting through the walls at all hours. On the other hand, for its devout regulars, this famous wrinkled old hotel has a tattered charm they love to romanticize. It is up to you which camp you are in.

English Spoken: Yes

Facilities and Services: Direct-dial phones, no elevator

Nearest Tourist Attractions (Left Bank): St-Germain-des-Prés, St-Michel, Île de la Cité, Île St-Louis

RATES
Single 200–280F, double 360–380F, triple 420F, quad 450F

BREAKFAST
Continental, included; cannot be deducted

Hôtel Saint-Germain-des-Prés ★★★
36, rue Bonaparte (6th)
30 rooms, all with bath or shower and toilet

The Saint-Germain-des-Prés is the kind of small hotel everyone hopes to find in Paris. Superbly located in the very *coeur* of St-Germain, it has a long history of famous guests. It began in 1778 as a Masonic lodge to which Voltaire, Benjamin Franklin, and U.S. Navy Captain John Paul Jones belonged. After it became a hotel, it housed philosopher Auguste Comte, American playwright Elmer Rice, and authors Henry Miller and Janet Flanner. Ms. Flanner lived here for years and wrote her "Letters from Paris" column for the *New Yorker* from her top-floor suite. The hotel's deserved popularity today is due in no small measure to the thoughtfulness of the staff members, who go to great lengths to cater to their guests, noting preferences in rooms and special interest.

The antiques and tapestry-filled salon overlooks a walled garden filled with masses of blooming hydrangeas and azaleas. The rooms are all stylishly decorated, and no two are alike. The suites are captivating, especially No. 26, which has Oriental rugs on polished wooden floors, a canopied bed, leaded glass windows, flower boxes, and a marble bath with Art Nouveau lights and fixtures.

Not content to rest on past laurels, the management is continually improving the hotel. Recently air-conditioning was added to all the rooms, a real bonus on hot days in this noisy section of Paris.

Everyone who stays here agrees that the Saint-Germain is definitely well worth the extra francs.

TELEPHONE
43-26-00-19

TELEX
200-409 F

FAX
(1) 40-46-83-63

MÉTRO
St-Germain-des-Prés

CREDIT CARDS
V

RATES
1 or 2 persons 700–800F, large double 1,050F, suite 1,650F; 200F extra per day for use of air-conditioning

BREAKFAST
Continental, included; cannot be deducted

English Spoken: Yes

Facilities and Services: Air-conditioning (add 200F per day), bar, direct-dial phones, elevator, hair dryers, mini-bars, private room safes, TVs, radios, room service

Nearest Tourist Attractions (Left Bank): St-Germain-des-Prés, Latin Quarter, Seine, Île de la Cité, Île St-Louis

Hôtel Saint-Michel ★
17, rue Git-le-Coeur (6th)

25 rooms, none with bath or shower or toilet

TELEPHONE
43-26-98-70

TELEX
None

FAX
None

MÉTRO
St-Michel

CREDIT CARDS
None; cash only

RATES
Single 195–290F, double 215–350F, triple 440F; hall shower 15F

BREAKFAST
Continental, included; cannot be deducted

This little down-and-out hotel is a great stop for students and young people with slim budgets and romantic notions about bohemian accommodations in Paris. Modest prices and the super location help to offset the basic rooms, none of which has a bath or toilet. Some of the rooms are definitely aged; others have received a fresh coat of paint in the not-too-distant past. A few have only hooks for closets, but all are clean. My advice is to inspect the room before accepting it. Night owls take note: The front door is closed and locked at 1 A.M., and no front-door keys are provided to the guests.

English Spoken: No, but Italian, Spanish, and Portuguese is

Facilities and Services: None

Nearest Tourist Attractions (Left Bank): St-Michel, St-Germain-des-Prés. Latin Quarter, Île de la Cité, Île St-Louis

Hôtel Saint-Paul ★★★
43, rue Monsieur-le-Prince (6th)

31 rooms, all with bath or shower and toilet

TELEPHONE
43-26-98-64

TELEX
203-257 F

FAX
(1) 46-34-58-60

MÉTRO
Odéon

CREDIT CARDS
AE, DC, MC, V

In the 17th century this building served as a hostel for Franciscan monks. For the last three generations, it has been a hotel owned by the Hawkins family. In 1987 they remodeled the hotel with elegant results, using the family's collection of impressive antiques, Oriental rugs, and watercolor paintings.

Custom-made curtains, fabric-covered walls, and some interesting brass beds combine with marble baths to create the pleasing rooms. One of my favorites is No. 51. Situated under the eaves, it has a cozy bedroom with a small sitting room and a bird's-eye view of the École de Médecine. For those insisting on total calm, No. 36 on the back is a pretty choice with its adorable brass bed, big bath, lovely old beams, and open window framing a big tree and a rooftop garden across the way.

English Spoken: Yes

Facilities and Services: Direct-dial phones, elevator, hair dryers, mini-bars, TVs, radios

Nearest Tourist Attractions (Left Bank): Luxembourg Gardens, St-Germain-des-Prés, St-Michel, Panthéon

RATES
Single 430F, double 500–700F, triple 750F, suite 1,000F; discounts offered July 15–Aug 30 and certain weekends

BREAKFAST
Continental, 40F (includes yogurt and juice)

Hôtel Saint-Pierre ★★
4, rue de l'École de Médecine (6th)

50 rooms, all with shower and sink; 25 with shower, sink, and toilet

If you want a central Latin Quarter location without spending big bucks to get it, the Saint-Pierre, next to the École de Médecine, is a smart Cheap Sleep. The unexceptional rooms will inspire you to leave early and return late, spending your time discovering Paris, not snoozing in your room. The rooms pay homage to the plain plastics and chenilles of the 1950s, but are clean and well maintained and have decent closet and luggage space. None has twin beds, all have a shower and sink, and half have private toilets. The hall facilities for those without are just fine. Management keeps a tight lid on loud voices, carry-in food, and non-paying guests in the rooms.

English Spoken: Yes

Facilities and Services: Elevator

Nearest Tourist Attractions (Left Bank): Latin Quarter, St-Michel, St-Germain-des-Prés, Île de la Cité, Île St-Louis, Luxembourg Gardens

TELEPHONE
46-34-78-80

TELEX
None

FAX
(1) 40-51-05-17

MÉTRO
Odéon

CREDIT CARDS
AE, DC, MC, V

RATES
Single 280–380F, double 340–420F, triple 440F

BREAKFAST
Continental, included (if you state at beginning of your stay that you will not take breakfast, 20F will be deducted from price of room)

L'Atelier Montparnasse Hôtel ★★★
49, rue Vavin (6th)

17 rooms, all with bath or shower and toilet

The present Montparnasse landscape of fast food

TELEPHONE
43-33-60-00

TELEX
203-255 F

FAX
(1) 40-51-04-21

MÉTRO
Vavin

CREDIT CARDS
AE, DC, MC, V

RATES
1 or 2 persons 580–810F; extra
bed 100F

BREAKFAST
Continental, 40F

restaurants, blockbuster movie theaters, and urban renewal almost makes one forget that this was once the artistic heart of Paris. The Atelier Montparnasse, designed by husband and wife team Frédéric and Diane Lionel du Pont, reminds guests of these past times by dedicating each floor of their renewed hotel to the work of a famous Montparnasse artist, including Modigliani, Foujita, and Picasso. Each of the plain, concise rooms has noise-proof double-paned windows, a mini-bar, a television, and a modern bathroom with a tiled mosaic behind the bathtub. The 1920s-inspired lobby has curved gray and blue walls, stunning Art Deco furniture, and an impressive display of contemporary original oil paintings. The hotel is within an easy walk to the Métro and the famous cafés and brasseries of Montparnasse.

English Spoken: Yes

Facilities and Services: Direct-dial phones, elevator, hair dryers, mini-bars, TVs with international reception

Nearest Tourist Attractions (Left Bank): Montparnasse, Luxembourg Gardens

Latitudes ★★★
7–11, rue St-Benoît (6th)

117 rooms, all with bath or shower and toilet

TELEPHONE
42-61-53-53

TELEX
213-531 F

FAX
(1) 49-27-09-33

MÉTRO
St-Germain-des-Prés, Mabillon

CREDIT CARDS
AE, DC, MC, V

RATES
Single 640–845F, double 735–
935F, triple 880–1,255F (rates
depend on season and whether
or not it is a corporate business
rate; always ask for lower rate)

BREAKFAST
Continental in room, buffet
downstairs; 60F

There is no question about it, Latitudes is one of the most sought-after three-star hotels on the Left Bank. Yes, it is part of a French hotel chain (the only link of this chain in Paris), and, yes, it costs more, but sometimes comfort, unsurpassed service, and convenience cost a bit more and are *worth* it.

On the main floor, the imposing marble-and-glass-lined lobby is as sophisticated as any in Paris. The piano bar has a live jazz band on weekends and during the week features different pianists. Complimentary newspapers are offered to guests enjoying a buffet breakfast in the sleek dining area. The extremely comfortable and attractive rooms are decorated in muted tones of rose, blue, and green. The premier rooms are the large corner doubles or those that join. The location is one of the best in the area for quality shopping, memorable strolling, and great restaurants in every price range (see *Cheap Eats in Paris*).

English Spoken: Yes

Facilities and Services: Piano bar with full bar service and live entertainment, bellhops, concierge, direct-dial phones, elevators, hair dryers, rooms for handicapped, room service, mini-bars, TVs with international reception, radios, clocks

    Nearest Tourist Attractions (Left Bank): St-Germain-des-Prés, Île de la Cité, Île St-Louis, St-Michel, shopping

Left Bank Hôtel ★★★
9, rue de l'Ancienne Comédie (6th)
31 rooms, all with bath or shower and toilet

It is hard to imagine a small hotel in Paris more appealing than the Left Bank Hôtel. Quite frankly, it is just the sort of hotel that will make anyone fall in love with Paris forever.

Located in the ever-popular St-Germain *quartier* and convenient to everything, it is beautifully run by the same owners who operate the Hôtel Lido in the eighth arrondissement (see page 110), so it is no surprise to find this one equally elegant and delightful. To add to the overall allure, there are fresh flowers everywhere, antique tapestries, polished antiques, ceiling beams, stone walls, and a helpful staff. The standard-sized rooms are done in paisley prints with built-in mini-bars and room safes. The bathrooms are excellent. However, for my hotel franc, the suites and larger doubles are the best bets, because they have alcove seating, soft armchairs, larger tiled baths, and loads of out-of-sight storage space. As you can tell, I am sold on this hotel as a good choice for those with more flexible budgets.

English Spoken: Yes

Facilities and Services: Air-conditioning, direct-dial phones, elevator, hair dryers, mini-bars, room safes, radios, clocks, TVs with international reception

    Nearest Tourist Attractions (Left Bank): St-Germain, Seine, Île de la Cité, St-Michel

TELEPHONE
43-54-01-70; toll free in the U.S. and Canada: 800-528-1234

TELEX
200-502 F

FAX
(1) 43-26-17-44

MÉTRO
Odéon

CREDIT CARDS
AE, DC, MC, V

RATES
Single 890F, double 1,000F, suite 1,155F

BREAKFAST
Continental, included; deduct 25F if not taken

Odéon Hôtel ★★★
3, rue de l'Odéon (6th)

TELEPHONE
43-25-90-67

TELEX
ODEOTEL 202-943 F

FAX
(1) 43-25-55-98

MÉTRO
Odéon

CREDIT CARDS
AE, DC, MC, V

RATES
Single 660–715F, double 715–935F

BREAKFAST
Continental, 45F

34 rooms, all with bath or shower and toilet

The Rue de l'Odéon was the first street in Paris to have pavement and gutters. At the turn of the century, French writers such as Paul Valéry, André Gide, and Paul Claudel lived nearby, and so did their Anglo-Saxon counterparts F. Scott Fitzgerald, Ernest Hemingway, James Joyce, and T.S. Eliot. Standing at No. 3 on this famous street is the Odéon Hôtel, which, like most other buildings here, is registered for its historic facade and rooflines.

Now owned and managed by the Fraenkel family, the hotel has great amounts of imagination and style. Each room displays Mme Fraenkel's sense of French taste and individuality. For instance, No. 630 has the original beams in both the bathroom and bedroom, a draped ceiling with matching fabric on the closet doors, a crisp white spread, and a peek-a-boo view of the Eiffel Tower. Number 629, on the top floor, is romantic and adorable with tiny windows, a pitched-beam ceiling, paisley-covered walls, and a gray and black marble bathroom. If traveling *toute seule*, No. 420, done with tiny rose provincial-print tissue on the walls and matching curtains, makes a cozy Parisian home.

The smartly updated entry and lounge has exposed weathered beams and offers low leather chairs and a long table where breakfast can be served if not taken in the room.

While the prices are steeper than some, this is a perfect solution for those who want a central St-Germain hotel with a quiet and almost sedate atmosphere.

English Spoken: Yes

Facilities and Services: Air-conditioned bedrooms, direct-dial phones, elevator, hair dryers, room safes, room service for drinks, radios, TVs

Nearest Tourist Attractions (Left Bank): St-Germain, Luxembourg Gardens

Pension de Famille Poirier (no stars)
120, boulevard Raspail (6th)

15 room and board rooms, 8 with bath or shower and toilet

Close to the Alliance Française and geared to students or those in Paris for the long haul, this family-run pension provides accommodations along with breakfast and a hot dinner Monday through Friday, a Saturday lunch, and a cold plate on Sunday. The homey decor on this second-floor lodging runs from tasteful to tacky in the pretty lounge with a television, to the basically functional rooms with an occasional antique and sagging bed. However, the good-natured youthful clientele doesn't seem to mind; they're too busy having fun in Paris, and who can blame them? The house rules are "just like those at home," a student informed me the day I visited. For example, there will be no surprise parties, no cooking in the rooms, no overnight guests of either sex, no visitors after 9:00 P.M., and definitely no feet on the tables. The rooms are cleaned every other day, the sheets are changed bimonthly (!), and clean towels are passed out once a week. For between-meal munch-outs, there is a refrigerator and microwave, and for sprucing up before a date or some other special event, an iron and ironing board are available. Between December 24 and January 2, no food or services are provided.

English Spoken: Not by management, but there is usually a bilingual student around

Facilities and Services: Elevator, room and board

Nearest Tourist Attractions (Left Bank): Alliance Française

TELEPHONE
45-48-24-15

TELEX
None

FAX
None

MÉTRO
Notre-Dame-des-Champs

CREDIT CARDS
None; cash only

RATES
Room and board: Single 210–260F daily, 5,300–6,000F monthly; double 340–360F daily, 8,000–9,000F monthly (includes breakfast, dinner Mon–Fri, Sat lunch, Sun cold plate); no charge for hall shower

Pension le Marronniers (no stars)
78, rue des Assas (6th)

12 rooms, none with bath or shower and toilet

For one of the most *incroyable* Cheap Sleeps in Paris, check into Mme Poirier's Pension les Marronniers. Her philanthropically low prices include not only a Continental breakfast, but a three-course dinner as well. With advance notice, she will

TELEPHONE
43-26-07-72 (reservations),
43-26-37-71 (pension guests)

TELEX
206-566 F, CODE 78

FAX
None

MÉTRO
Vavin, Notre-Dame-des-
Champs
CREDIT CARDS
None; cash only
RATES
Single 160–250F, double
350F, triple 435F; monthly
rates: single 3,600F–6,300F,
double 8,600F, triple 10,500F
BREAKFAST
Continental, included (as is
dinner); cannot be deducted

cater to special dietary preferences. Students, French-men in from the provinces doing a work/study program, and smart budgeteers fill her third-floor walk-up home, which has the Laura Ashley decorating seal of approval in the dining and living rooms, complete with house mascot, the big dog Lamoute, asleep in the most comfortable chair or sunniest spot. The bedrooms might seem a bit primitive to many, but all are cleaned every other day, and the linens are changed weekly. Reservations are absolutely essential months in advance. Madame prefers guests who stay a long time; meals are part of the program and cannot be deducted for any reason.

English Spoken: Some; many guests speak English

Facilities and Services: Breakfast and dinner included in price

Nearest Tourist Attractions (Left Bank): Luxembourg Gardens, St-Germain-des-Prés, Alliance Française

Regent's Hôtel ★★
44, rue Madame (6th)

TELEPHONE
45-48-02-81
TELEX
None
FAX
(1) 45-44-85-73
MÉTRO
St-Sulpice, Rennes
CREDIT CARDS
MC, V
RATES
1 or 2 persons 440–590F; extra
bed 110F
BREAKFAST
Continental, 40F

37 rooms, all with bath or shower and toilet

The Regents Hôtel is a snug, safe spot in the vicinity of Luxembourg Gardens, with quick and easy access to St-Germain, Montparnasse, and hardcore discount shopping on Rue St-Placide by the Bon Marché department store (see "Cheap Chic" discount shopping, page 163). One of the prettiest features of this hotel is the patio. With its beds of flowers and white wrought-iron furniture, it is a nice place to have a leisurely breakfast or to meet other guests and compare Parisian notes.

The clean rooms are as plain as can be, with a smattering of orange mixed with red and rust. The furniture is *faux rustique,* and chenille is the fabric of choice. There are several large family rooms that offer good value. Owner Daniel Cretey is on board daily, running a tight but friendly operation.

English Spoken: Yes

Facilities and Services: Direct-dial phones, elevator

Nearest Tourist Attractions (Left Bank): Luxem-

bourg Gardens, St-Germain, discount shopping near
Bon Marché department store

Villa des Artistes ★★★
9, rue de la Grande Chaumière (6th)
59 rooms, all with bath or shower and toilet

For years the old Hôtel Liberia occupied this spot as a faded, *très passé* fleabag shrine to backpackers and those down on their luck and travel budgets—but no longer is this the case. Thanks to a stunning total-renovation project that even included a new name, the Villa des Artistes now can be described as a bright light on the Montparnasse hotel scene. Under the umbrella of Best Western in France, it has been quickly adopted by businessmen and travelers wanting a full-service hotel in this area. One of the major focal points of the hotel's new look is a handsome inner garden to one side of a glass-walled dining room where a breakfast buffet is served each morning. The accommodations either overlook the street or this cleverly done garden courtyard, where the half-trellised walls lined with green plants are painted above with cloud murals to hide an otherwise dreary view. Each unit exhibits comfortable and efficient decor in shades of maroon with light-wood built-ins and the latest in marble bathrooms.

English Spoken: Yes

Facilities and Services: Direct-dial phones, elevator, hair dryers, mini-bars in more expensive rooms, room safes, radios, TVs

Nearest Tourist Attractions (Left Bank): Montparnasse, Luxembourg Gardens

TELEPHONE
43-26-60-86; toll free in U.S. and Canada; 800-528-1234

TELEX
204-080 F

FAX
(1) 43-54-73-70

MÉTRO
Vavin

CREDIT CARDS
AE, DC, MC, V

RATES
1 or 2 persons 600–810F; extra bed 160F

BREAKFAST
Continental, included; cannot be deducted

Welcome Hôtel ★★
66, rue de Seine, corner of Boulevard
St-Germain (6th)
30 rooms, all with bath or shower and toilet

Unpretentious rooms in a fun-filled location combine with moderate prices to make a stay here more than welcome. Composed of thirty rooms on six floors, this friendly spot on the corner of Rue de Seine and Boulevard St-Germain is directly across from the

TELEPHONE
46-34-24-80

TELEX
None

FAX
(1) 40-46-81-59

MÉTRO
Odéon, Mabillon, St-Germain-des-Prés

CREDIT CARDS
None; cash only

RATES
Single 335–500F, double 480–500F

BREAKFAST
Continental, 35F

picturesque Rue de Buci street *marché*. Because many of the rooms are on the small side, it is an especially suitable stopover for singles. Those wanting more spacious accommodations should ask for No. 52, a corner twin-bedded room, or No. 62, an attic nest with beams and a peaked ceiling. In the past year the ragged edges that kept the hotel out of the last edition of *Cheap Sleeps in Paris* have been smoothed out, and new paint has brightened the rooms and hallways. It is admittedly still *very* noisy, and the top floor rooms can be stuffy and hot in warm weather, but these drawbacks can be overlooked because of the super location. The hotel is within walking distance of more things to see and do than you will finish in a week. The *quartier* has scores of inexpensive eating places (see *Cheap Eats in Paris*), and shoppers will never finish browsing or wishing.

English Spoken: Yes

Facilities and Services: Direct-dial phones, elevator, TVs

Nearest Tourist Attractions (Left Bank): St-Germain, Seine, Île de la Cité, Île St-Louis, St-Michel, Luxembourg Gardens, great shopping

SEVENTH ARRONDISSEMENT

SEVENTH ARRONDISSEMENT
Left Bank: Champ-de-Mars, École Militaire, Eiffel Tower, Invalides, Musée de Orsay, Rodin Museum, UNESCO

Known affectionately as "Seventh Heaven," this quiet, beautiful residential area is full of lovely mansions built before the Revolution and now occupied by embassies or government offices. The Champ-de-Mars served as the parade ground for the École Militaire and is the backyard of the Eiffel Tower. Les Invalides is the home of four world-famous military museums and is the final resting place of Napoléon Bonaparte.

HOTELS IN THE SEVENTH ARRONDISSEMENT
Eiffel Park Hôtel ★★★
Grand Hôtel Lévêque ★
Hôtel Amélie ★★
Hôtel Bersoly's Saint-Germain ★★★

Hôtel de l'Académie ★★★
Hôtel de Londres ★★★
Hôtel de l'Université ★★★
Hôtel de Nevers ★★
Hôtel de Suède ★★★
Hôtel Duc de Saint-Simon ★★★
Hôtel du Champ de Mars ★★
Hôtel du Palais Bourbon ★★
Hôtel Élysées Maubourg ★★★
Hôtel la Bourdonnais ★★★
Hôtel les Jardins d'Eiffel ★★★
Hôtel Muguet ★★
Hôtel Saint-Dominique ★★
Hôtel Saint-Thomas d'Aquin ★★
Hôtel Saxe Résidence ★★★
Hôtel Solférino ★★
Résidence Latour Maubourg ★★

Eiffel Park Hôtel ★★★
17 bis, rue Amélie (7th)

36 rooms, all with bath or shower and toilet

An up-to-the-minute atmosphere in a terrace suite with chocolates on your pillow every night—sounds heavenly, doesn't it? Check into the Eiffel Park Hôtel in the seventh arrondissement, and all this and more will be yours.

A large mirror-lined elevator takes you to your room, which is done in a mixture of yellows and cornflower blue. In the afternoon, relax on the roof-top terrace with its view of the top of the Eiffel Tower and return to your room via the impressive glassed-in stairway. In the evening, drinks are served in the engaging downstairs lobby bar, which displays the latest in modern Italian furnishings.

This hotel was created from scratch by a dynamic young team that spared no expense or effort to provide for the comfort of guests. Located on a very peaceful side street, but close to many good restaurants, discount shopping, and the Eiffel Tower, it is hard to imagine a stay here being anything but wonderful.

English Spoken: Yes

TELEPHONE
45-55-10-01

TELEX
202-950 F

FAX
(1) 47-05-28-68

MÉTRO
Latour-Maubourg

CREDIT CARDS
AE, DC, MC, V

RATES
Single 655F, double 680–750F, suite 900F

BREAKFAST
Continental, 40F

Facilities and Services: Bar, conference room, direct-dial phones, elevator, hair dryers, mini-bars, room safes, TVs with international reception, radios, same-day laundry service

Nearest Tourist Attractions (Left Bank): Champ-de-Mars, Eiffel Tower, Invalides, good shopping

Grand Hôtel Lévêque ★
29, rue Cler (7th)

50 rooms, 25 with bath or shower and toilet

TELEPHONE
47-05-49-15

TELEX
None

FAX
(1) 45-50-49-36

MÉTRO
École Militaire, Latour-Maubourg

CREDIT CARDS
Prefer cash; will accept Visa

RATES
1 or 2 persons 190–320F, 3 persons 390F; hall shower free

BREAKFAST
Continental (no croissants), 25F

Committed Cheap Sleepers who like the seventh arrondissement will love the redone Lévêque. Located among the colorful food shops that line the Rue Cler, it is close to all the things that one often forgets are so important on a trip: banks, a post office, do-it-yourself laundries, cleaners, cafés for a mid-morning cup of hot chocolate, a street *marché,* and several exceptional cheese shops and *charcuteries* for low-cost snacks.

The refurbishing project, which was long overdue, breathed new life into the hotel, and it is now a spiffy choice and firmly recommended. Despite the use of chenille, some marginal-quality furniture, and limited lighting, the rooms are clean and the mattresses just like cement. If you have a bathless room, the showers in the hall are free and the toilets spotless. The hotel is enjoying renewed popularity, so if you are interested, book ahead at least one month during busy times.

English Spoken: Limited

Facilities and Services: Direct-dial phones, no elevator

Nearest Tourist Attractions (Left Bank): Champ-de-Mars park, Eiffel Tower, good shopping, lively street *marché*

Hôtel Amélie ★★
5, rue Amélie (7th)

15 rooms, all with bath or shower and toilet

TELEPHONE
45-51-74-75

TELEX
None

FAX
(1) 45-56-93-55

Cute, clean, and cheap for the area, the Amélie has none of the usual violent colors or dime-store taste found in so many other two-star hotels in Paris. True, the rooms and closets are pocket-sized, but they are freshly decorated in whites and pastels and have tiled bathrooms with decent showers. Breakfast is served in a miniature sitting room on the first landing, or in bed if that is your choice. Great restaurants line the neighborhood (see *Cheap Eats in Paris*), and tempting discount shopping on Rue St-Dominique is only a minute away (see "Cheap Chic," page 163). The new owners, M. and Mme Orville, speak English, and *en plus*—they love Americans!

English Spoken: Yes

Facilities and Services: Direct-dial phones, no elevator, mini-bars, TVs

Nearest Tourist Attractions (Left Bank): Invalides, Seine, Eiffel Tower, Champ-de-Mars, discount shopping

MÉTRO
Latour-Maubourg

CREDIT CARDS
AE, DC, MC, V

RATES
Single 320F, double 380–400F, triple 470F

BREAKFAST
Continental, 35F

Hôtel Bersoly's Saint-Germain ★★★
28, rue de Lille (7th)
16 rooms, all with bath or shower and toilet

A smart restoration transformed the interior of this once-dilapidated 16th-century hotel into an artistic fantasy. The decorators kept the original steep stairway leading to the cellar breakfast rooms, one done bistro style and the other in an Oriental motif. The old stone walls and floors in the lobby have been cleaned and restored, and an atrium garden with blooming plants has been added, giving color to the main floor.

To set the hotel apart from many like it in the area, every bedroom has been named for a famous artist. In each case, a reproduction of one of that artist's paintings hangs in the room, and the mood and color scheme of the room are taken from the painting. If you like bold reds and black, request the ground-floor Picasso room, with its entrance off the atrium garden. Or, if you prefer pastels, the Seurat or the Sisley room is the one to ask for. Small bathrooms, low seating in the rooms, and the steep steps may discourage some. Others will love the peaceful location, only minutes away from the Musée d'Orsay, the Louvre, serious shopping, and equally serious restaurants (see *Cheap Eats in Paris*).

English Spoken: Yes

TELEPHONE
42-60-73-79

TELEX
217-505 F

FAX
(1) 49-27-05-55

MÉTRO
Rue du Bac, St-Germain-des-Prés

CREDIT CARDS
MC, V

RATES
1 or 2 persons 525–675F

BREAKFAST
Continental, 40F

Facilities and Services: Bar, direct-dial phones, elevator to 4th floor only, hair dryers, TVs, room fans in summer, light snacks served

Nearest Tourist Attractions (Left Bank): Musée d'Orsay, Louvre, Tuileries, Seine, shopping

Hôtel de l'Académie ★★★
32, rue des Saints-Pères (7th)

TELEPHONE
45-48-36-22

TELEX
205-650 F

FAX
(1) 45-44-75-24

MÉTRO
St-Germain-des-Prés

CREDIT CARDS
AE, DC, MC, V

RATES
1 or 2 persons 625–725F

BREAKFAST
Continental, 45F

34 rooms, all with bath or shower and toilet

Sheltered in yet another deftly restored 17th-century building on the Left Bank, this attractive hotel was once the residence for the private guards of the Duc de Rohan. Intact in the public areas are the original ceilings and stone walls, highlighted by Oriental rugs, country French furniture, and colorful dried flower arrangements. The small but well-decorated rooms have coordinating window treatments and bedspreads in either pink or blue floral print. The bathrooms are nicely tiled and supplied with French toiletries and good towels. The hotel is on the edge of St-Germain and within a brisk walk of the Musée d'Orsay, Notre-Dame, and many recommendable restaurants (see *Cheap Eats in Paris*).

English Spoken: Yes

Facilities and Services: Bar, direct-dial phones, elevator, hair dryers, mini-bars, radios, TVs with international reception

Nearest Tourist Attractions (Left Bank): Good walk to Musée d'Orsay, islands, Seine, St-Germain

Hôtel de Londres ★★★
1, rue Augereau (7th)

TELEPHONE
45-51-63-02

TELEX
206-398 F HOTLONDR

FAX
(1) 47-05-28-96

MÉTRO
École Militaire

CREDIT CARDS
AE, DC, MC, V

30 rooms, all with bath or shower and toilet

Realistic prices, a quiet location in a French bourgeois neighborhood, easy walking distance from the Eiffel Tower, colorful shopping, and a good Métro connection—all make this a fine selection if you don't require loads of space.

A soothing color scheme of beiges, browns, and soft blues creates a tranquil mood in the exceptionally clean and well-maintained bedrooms. Closet space is limited, and the tiled baths are tiny but functional.

Two of the top-floor rooms have peeking views of the Eiffel Tower, but a few on the first floor are stuffy any time of the year and should be avoided. Off the reception area is a garden breakfast room that is a delightful place to read the morning *International Herald-Tribune* over a café au lait. The desk staff is outstanding, and management is on the scene throughout the day, keeping everything running well.

English Spoken: Yes

Facilities and Services: Direct-dial phones, elevator in main building, hair dryers, mini-bars, TVs, radios

Nearest Tourist Attractions (Left Bank): Champ-de-Mars, Eiffel Tower, Invalides, Seine, good shopping

RATES
1 or 2 persons 340–590F, 3 persons 735F; extra bed 145F
BREAKFAST
Continental, 35F

Hôtel de l'Université ★★★
22, rue de l'Université (7th)
22 rooms, all with bath or shower and toilet

Despite its rather steep rates, l'Université is booked solid months ahead with people who want to stay in a very personalized small hotel a block from Boulevard St-Germain and minutes from the Louvre and the Musée d'Orsay. Many restored *hôtel particuliers* have little room to breathe in their enticing but *trés petite* rooms. This hotel is an exception. Even though the rooms vary in shape and size, all are graced with the owner's personal collection of fine antiques. Each comfortable room comes with a good-sized bathroom, a nice chair, and a large table, and has plenty of space for two people to settle in. The rooms on the fourth floor have pretty Left Bank views; others have private terraces with seasonal potted plants, and one has a fireplace.

A small bistro-style breakfast room opens onto a tiny courtyard with a fountain. Service from all members of the staff is outgoing and friendly.

English Spoken: Yes

Facilities and Services: Bar (open Mon–Fri), direct-dial phones, elevator to all but top floor, mini-bars (except in singles), room service, light snacks, room safes, TVs

TELEPHONE
42-61-09-39
TELEX
260-717 OREM 310
FAX
(1) 42-60-40-84
MÉTRO
Rue du Bac
CREDIT CARDS
None; cash only
RATES
Single 440–660F, double 660–1,430F, triple 770–1,430F
BREAKFAST
Continental, 50F

Nearest Tourist Attractions (Left Bank): Musée d'Orsay, Louvre, Seine, St-Germain-des-Prés, interesting shopping

Hôtel de Nevers ★★
83, rue du Bac (7th)

TELEPHONE
45-44-61-30

TELEX
None

FAX
(1) 42-22-29-47

MÉTRO
Rue du Bac

CREDIT CARDS
None; cash only

RATES
Single 330F, double 400–420F; extra bed 80F

BREAKFAST
Continental 30F (includes juice and yogurt)

11 rooms, all with bath or shower and toilet

For price, location, and a sense of *vieux* Paris, this neat little hotel of dollhouse proportions stands head and shoulders above its nearest rival. If you do decide to stay here, you can have all sorts of fun spending the money you saved in one of the boutiques or antiques shops that this neighborhood is so famous for.

Appealing to fashionable and pretty guests on the way up, the tiny bedrooms are individually named after country flowers. I like No. 11, "Clématite," on the fourth floor with a private roof terrace and a view of slate roofs and red chimney pots that seems to go on forever. Number 10, "Campanule," is also appealing, with a small patio and a big skylight opening from the pitched roof. There is no elevator, and *le petit déjeuner* is served in a miniscule top-floor salon that is a nice climb up a winding stone stairwell.

English Spoken: Yes

Facilities and Services: Direct-dial phones, no elevator, mini-bars in some rooms

Nearest Tourist Attractions (Left Bank): Musée d'Orsay, Seine, St-Germain-des-Prés, good shopping

Hôtel de Suède ★★★
31, rue Vaneau (7th)

TELEPHONE
47-05-00-08

TELEX
200-596 F

FAX
(1) 47-05-69-27

MÉTRO
St-François Xavier

CREDIT CARDS
AE, MC, V

37 rooms, all with bath or shower and toilet, 4 singles with no bath, shower, or toilet

While the Suède has no flamboyance, it has a conservative elegance that makes it outstanding in its class. No one talks about the hotel, probably because it is sequestered in a quiet embassy *quartier* adjoining the Matignon Gardens, the residence of the French prime minister.

Everything about the hotel suggests a dignified traditionalism, which appeals to its venerable clientele. The wood-paneled lobby has clusters of soft velvet couches and chairs, creating inviting places to meet a friend or join other guests for cocktails. The rooms are uniformly done in blue and gray velvet, with built-in closets and writing desks, two easy chairs, and luxurious carpeting. The rooms overlooking the Matignon Gardens are the nicest. Those to avoid are the depressing ground-floor units, which are dark and airless. A uniformed staff provides professional services, from bartending to room service. A full breakfast menu is available, as are sandwiches and light snacks. The area is somewhat remote from public transportation, but it is not hard to find street parking if you are driving your own car.

English Spoken: Yes

Facilities and Services: Bar, direct-dial phones, elevator, room service for light snacks, TVs on request

Nearest Tourist Attractions (Left Bank): Rodin Museum, Musée d'Orsay

RATES
Single (no facilities) 235F, single with full facilites 535F, double 585–825F, triple 795F, suite/apartment 1,030F; shower 20F

BREAKFAST
Continental, included; cannot be deducted

Hôtel Duc de Saint-Simon ★★★
14, rue de Saint-Simon (7th)

34 rooms, all with bath or shower and toilet

Everyone has a first hotel in Paris, and this was mine. Over the years my enthusiasm for it has not dimmed, and it still tops my short list of ideal small Parisian hotels.

I am drawn to the Duc de Saint-Simon for many reasons, especially its intimately romantic feeling, wonderful sense of privacy, and high degree of personalized service. Built around a courtyard garden, many of the rooms open onto this green view, while several larger rooms and suites open onto their own private terraces. I like *all* the rooms, but a favorite is No. 11, decorated in rich floral fabrics with a corner sitting area and view windows that open to the gardens and seem to bring them inside.

The owners of the hotel, M. and Mme Lindqvist, have been country French antiques collectors of note for many years and have used their handsome collection throughout the hotel, from the beautiful grandfather clock in the lobby to the graceful marble-topped dressers in the bedrooms. The downstairs

TELEPHONE
45-48-35-66, 42-22-07-52 for reservations

TELEX
203-277 F

FAX
(1) 45-48-68-25

MÉTRO
Rue du Bac

CREDIT CARDS
None; cash only

RATES
1 or 2 persons 1,000–1,420F, suite/apartment 1,470–1,840F

BREAKFAST
Continental, 65F

cellar bar has pillowed niches and quiet corners just big enough for two to sip drinks and talk about life and love.

The prices for a stay here are high, no doubt about it. But for those seeking a quietly elegant and discreet stay in Paris, this should be *the* hotel of choice.

English Spoken: Yes

Facilities and Services: Bar, direct-dial phones, elevator, hair dryers, light snacks, porter, room service, some air-conditioned rooms, TVs

Nearest Tourist Attractions (Left Bank): Musée d'Orsay, Tuileries, St-Germain-des-Prés, Rodin Museum, Invalides, excellent browsing and shopping

Hôtel du Champ de Mars ★★
7, rue Champ-de-Mars (7th)
24 rooms, all with bath or shower and toilet

TELEPHONE
45-51-52-30

TELEX
None

FAX
None

MÉTRO
École Militaire

CREDIT CARDS
MC. V

RATES
Single 370F, double 370–400F, triple 475F

BREAKFAST
Continental, 35F

French tourists visiting their capital have discovered this remarkable hotel value located between the Eiffel Tower and Invalides. This modest but modern and fastidiously maintained hotel reflects great pride of ownership. The lobby showcases the owners' impressive collection of begonias and stag-horn ferns, and other signs of their green thumbs are evident throughout the rest of the hotel.

The quiet, updated rooms have simple, harmonious color schemes, rustic wooden furniture, and firm mattresses. Rooms No. 2 and 4 have their own small garden and are especially appealing during the summer months. The rooms along the back are very quiet, but have little light and depressing views of blank walls. The homey downstairs breakfast room has a color TV where you can catch up on the morning news by watching *Bonjour France*. Excellent discount shopping, several banks, a main post office, the Métro, and lots of favorite Cheap Eats in Paris are all close at hand.

English Spoken: No

Facilities and Services: Direct-dial phones, elevator

Nearest Tourist Attractions (Left Bank): Champ-de-Mars, Eiffel Tower, Invalides, good discount shopping, interesting daily street *marché*, Seine

Hôtel du Palais Bourbon ★★
49, rue de Bourgogne (7th)

34 rooms, 29 with bath or shower and toilet

Long a favorite with readers of *Cheap Sleeps in Paris* looking for a clean and respectable hotel suitable for the entire family, the Palais Bourbon continues to be impossible to top. Located in a quiet residential area of Paris only one-half block from the Rodin Museum, five minutes from Les Invalides, and about ten from the Musée d'Orsay, it is just across the Seine from the Tuileries.

The downstairs areas are filled with antiques belonging to the Claudon family, who have owned, managed, and lived in the hotel for almost 50 years. The huge 1950s-style bedrooms are only slightly less than austere, but antiseptically clean and spacious enough for children to play in. Plans are now in the works for renovating at least four rooms per year, and I am sure that Mme Claudon will see to it that they are very nice.

English Spoken: Limited

Facilities and Services: Direct-dial phones, elevator, mini-bars, TVs in rooms that have bathtubs

Nearest Tourist Attractions (Left Bank): Rodin Museum, Invalides, Musée d'Orsay, Seine, Tuileries

TELEPHONE
45-51-63-32, 47-05-29-26

TELEX
PB 205 746 F

FAX
(1) 45-55-20-21

MÉTRO
Varenne, Invalides, Chambre des Députés

CREDIT CARDS
MC, V

RATES
Single 176F (no facilities)–265F, double 217F (no facilities)–410F, triple 540F; extra bed, add 30%

BREAKFAST
Continental, included; cannot be deducted

Hôtel Élysées Maubourg ★★★
35, boulevard Latour-Maubourg (7th)

30 rooms, all with bath or shower and toilet

The Best Western–aligned Élysées Maubourg is a favorite stopping place for those seeking serene surroundings and superior service from a professional hotel staff. In addition to the 30 well-fitted rooms, it boasts a Finnish sauna that is free for guests to use at their leisure. The traditionally styled rooms are decorated without much originality, but they are superbly comfortable, with plenty of space and good bathrooms with modern accessories. Business-people will appreciate the location, which has good bus and Métro connections as well as taxi stands close by. The nicely appointed lobby and the stone cellar breakfast room

TELEPHONE
45-56-10-78; toll free from U.S. and Canada: 800-528-1234

TELEX
206-227 F

FAX
(1) 47-05-65-08

MÉTRO
Latour-Maubourg

CREDIT CARDS
AE, DC, MC, V

RATES
Single 550F, double 660–815F

BREAKFAST
Continental, 35F

with its marble-topped bistro tables and matching chairs are additional pleasures.

English Spoken: Yes

Facilities and Services: Bar, conference room, direct-dial phones, elevator, hair dryers, mini-bars, room safes, radios, TVs with international reception

Nearest Tourist Attractions (Left Bank): Invalides, Rodin Museum

Hôtel la Bourdonnais ★★★
111, 113 avenue de la Bourdonnais (7th)
60 rooms, all with bath or shower and toilet

TELEPHONE
47-05-45-42
TELEX
201-416 F
FAX
(1) 45-55-75-54
MÉTRO
École Militaire
CREDIT CARDS
DC, MC, V
RATES
Single 450F, double 520–580F, triple 610F, quad 650F
BREAKFAST
Continental, 28F

Hôtel la Bourdonnais is a personal favorite that over the years has never failed to please. The location could not be better. It is five minutes from a Métro and only ten from a RER stop. The area is filled with good shopping of all kinds, from discount clothing boutiques to a lively daily street *marché*. There are many inexpensive restaurants within easy walking distance (see *Cheap Eats in Paris*). The beautiful Champ-de-Mars park, with the Eiffel Tower at one end and the impressive École Militaire at the other, is only two blocks away and a great place for a picnic, people-watching, or a morning jog.

The serene lobby and reception rooms are accented by soft lighting, bouquets of flowers, and nice paintings. A small breakfast salon and bar overlook a glassed-in garden where drinks and *petit dejeuner* are served. The crisply maintained rooms are tastefully decorated with period furniture and soft fabrics. All have very generous closets, comfortable chairs, large writing desks, and hidden combination safes to store valuables. The large marble bathrooms feature big mirrors, hair dryers, and lots of towels. This hotel is the choice of many international travelers, so reserve way ahead to avoid disappointment.

English Spoken: Yes

Facilities and Services: Bar, restaurant (expensive), direct-dial phones, elevator, porter, hair dryers, mini-bars, room safes, radios, TVs with international reception

Nearest Tourist Attractions (Left Bank): Champ-de-Mars, Eiffel Tower, Invalides, Trocadéro, Seine, good shopping

Hôtel les Jardins d'Eiffel ★★★
8, rue Amélie (7th)
44 rooms, all with bath or shower and toilet

Les Jardins d'Eiffel sings with style from top to bottom as it continues to be a favorite in the *quartier* between the Invalides and the Eiffel Tower. In the few years it has been open, it has built a solid reputation as a luxurious small hotel offering many four-star features at three-star prices.

After a hard day, you can park your car in the hotel garage, work out in the hotel gym or relax in the sauna, then wander a block in almost any direction and find a wonderful restaurant serving food you will love at prices you can afford (See *Cheap Eats in Paris*).

The quiet rooms and suites are elegantly and comfortably designed. A pretty breakfast dining room overlooks a garden terrace. Each month the management invites local artists to display their work in the main salon, then asks hotel guests to a cocktail party to meet the artists and to have an opportunity to purchase their work. The professional desk staff will book dinner or theater reservations, organize sightseeing trips, rent a car for you with or without a driver, and confirm airline tickets. There is a one-day laundry and cleaning service and a doctor is on call 24 hours a day.

English Spoken: Yes

Facilities and Services: Bar, conference room, direct-dial phones, elevator, hair dryers, mini-bars, TVs with international reception, radios, clocks, room safes, trouser presses, private parking, gym, babysitters, full concierge services, one-day laundry and dry cleaning, doctor on 24-hour call

Nearest Tourist Attractions (Left Bank): Champ-de-Mars, Invalides, Eiffel Tower, good shopping

TELEPHONE
47-05-46-21

TELEX
206-582 F

FAX
(1) 45-55-28-08

MÉTRO
Latour-Maubourg

CREDIT CARDS
AE, DC, MC, V

RATES
Rates depend on season: Single 500–680F, double 600–800F, triple 750–950F, suite 1,100–1,520F; sauna 70F, garage 85F

BREAKFAST
Continental, 45F

Hôtel Muguet ★★
11, rue Chevert (7th)
43 rooms, 17 with bath or shower and toilet

TELEPHONE
47-05-05-93
TELEX
None
FAX
(1) 45-50-25-37
MÉTRO
École Militaire
CREDIT CARDS
AE. MC, V
RATES
Single 200–350F, double 250–
350F, hall shower 15F
BREAKFAST
Continental (served in room
only), 30F

Hidden on an out-of-the-way street, this old-fashioned cheapie hasn't changed much over the years. The 1950s-style rooms make no pretense at haute decor, but they are unusually spacious and squeaky clean. It is important to note that only one room has twin beds, and the only shower is on the sixth floor. The owners reside at the hotel and oversee every detail, from riding herd on the cleaning staff to discouraging drip-dry laundries. Because they don't speak English, they have developed an understanding attitude toward struggling French speakers.

The immediate neighborhood is rather dull, but very quiet both day and night. After a nice ten-minute walk you can be at the Invalides viewing Napoléon's tomb, on a park bench at the Champ-de-Mars park admiring the Eiffel Tower, or on the Métro on your way to another part of Paris.

English Spoken: No

Facilities and Services: Direct-dial phones, elevator

Nearest Tourist Attractions (Left Bank): Champ-de-Mars, Invalides, Eiffel Tower, UNESCO, Rodin Museum

Hôtel Saint-Dominique ★★
62, rue St-Dominique (7th)
34 rooms, all with bath or shower and toilet

TELEPHONE
47-05-51-44
TELEX
206-968 F
FAX
(1) 47-05-81-28
MÉTRO
Latour-Maubourg
CREDIT CARDS
AE, DC, MC, V
RATES
Single 455–495F, double 455–
610F, triple 670F
BREAKFAST
Continental, 40F

In the 1700s, the building housed Dominican nuns. Today, it is a quaint hotel on a busy shopping street. An English country theme is carried out from the beamed lobby to the snug rooms, which are furnished in hand-rubbed pine and wicker, with soft, billowing curtains dressing the windows. Matching spreads, coordinated wall coverings, and pile carpeting add further appeal. My favorite rooms are the two new ones, which open onto the garden terrace where breakfast is served on warm spring and summer mornings. The rooms do not boast exciting views, and the elevator does not service all floors, but for a comfortable and tranquil stay with reasonable rates, this hotel can be recommended.

English Spoken: Yes

Facilities and Services: Direct-dial phones, eleva-

tor to most floors, some hair dryers, mini-bars, room safes, TV with international reception

Nearest Tourist Attractions (Left Bank): Invalides, Champ-de-Mars, Eiffel Tower, Rodin Museum, good shopping

Hôtel Saint-Thomas d'Aquin ★★
3, rue du Pré-aux-Clercs (7th)
21 rooms, all with bath, shower, and toilet

In an area where prices and noise are generally quite high, the Saint-Thomas d'Aquin is a moderate choice. The modern, unsophisticated interior in chrome, Formica, and Naugahyde leaves me a little cold, but the glistening rooms are efficently arranged and exceptionally well kept. The competent English-speaking managers are diligent and friendly, which has encouraged repeat guests who have been loyal to the hotel for many years. The location couldn't be better. The Musée d'Orsay, Louvre, Tuileries, and all of St-Germain-des-Prés are within a 10-to-20-minute walk. The shopping is wonderful, and so are many restaurants in the neighborhood (see *Cheap Eats in Paris*).

English Spoken: Yes

Facilities and Services: Direct-dial phones, elevator, TVs

Nearest Tourist Attractions (Left Bank): Musée d'Orsay, Louvre, St-Germain-des-Prés, shopping

TELEPHONE
42-61-01-22

TELEX
None

FAX
(1) 42-61-41-43

MÉTRO
St-Germain-des-Prés

CREDIT CARDS
AE, DC, MC, V

RATES
Single 420–490F, double 460–525F, triple 665F

BREAKFAST
Continental, included; cannot be deducted

Hôtel Saxe Résidence ★★★
9, Villa de Saxe (7th)
52 rooms, all with bath or shower and toilet

If you want glamor and glitter in an exciting part of Paris, better keep right on looking. If, on the other hand, you are a Paris veteran with a car and enjoy hearing birds singing rather than horns honking, this 52-room hotel is a good choice. Hidden at the end of a cul-de-sac in a tourist-free corner of the seventh arrondissement, the hotel has the rather cool and businesslike character of a basic Holiday Inn.

The conventional 1960s-style rooms have small entry halls, resulting in a feeling of spaciousness. All

TELEPHONE
47-83-98-28

TELEX
270-139 F SAXOTEL

FAX
(1) 47-83-85-47

MÉTRO
Ségur

CREDIT CARDS
AE, DC, MC, V

RATES
1 or 2 persons 580F, 3 persons
735F, 4 persons 780F, suite
780F

BREAKFAST
Continental, 35F

are comfortably fitted with armchairs, built-in desks, and good closet and luggage space—important pluses for longer stays. There are nice views from almost every room, some over the elegant apartment residences for which this neighborhood is known, and others over the trees and green spaces nearby or the convent next door. A young and energetic new manager, Mme Florence Fouan, has vastly improved the caliber of service, from the attitude of the front desk staff to the housekeeping standards of the cleaning crew. The only drawback, really, is the deadly dull neighborhood, which has no tourist sites or restaurants inside of a 10-to-15-minute walk.

English Spoken: Yes

Facilities and Services: Bar, conference room, direct-dial phones, elevator, hair dryers, mini-bars, free parking for 5 cars, private safe, radios, TVs with international reception

Nearest Tourist Attraction (Left Bank): Champ-de-Mars, Eiffel Tower, UNESCO, Invalides, Rodin Museum

Hôtel Solférino ★★
91, rue de Lille (7th)

TELEPHONE
47-05-85-54

TELEX
203-865 F

FAX
(1) 45-55-51-16

MÉTRO
Solférino, RER-Musée d'Orsay

CREDIT CARDS
MC, V

RATES
Single 265–445F, double 475–
645F

BREAKFAST
Continental, 30F; included

33 rooms, 28 with bath or shower and toilet

The Solférino is a top choice for Cheap Sleepers in search of a sedate location, delightfully situated just off the Seine and near the historic Palais de la Légion de l'Honneur and the Musée d'Orsay.

Decorated with an eclectic flair, the hotel mixes antiques, paintings, and curios in a cheerful nonconventional way. Dining in the sunny breakfast room with its skylight, display of hand-painted ceramics, and potted flowers and plants is like eating in a spring garden. The no-nonsense bedrooms are adequate, from the tiny bathless top-floor singles to the larger doubles equipped with showers and toilets. Every effort is made to maintain the rooms, and they all pass the white-glove test. Guests are treated warmly by the congenial owner and her multilingual staff, and, as a result, there are many who return.

English Spoken: Yes

Facilities and Services: Direct-dial phones, elevator to all but top floor, TVs available for 200F per week

Nearest Tourist Attractions (Left Bank): Musée d'Orsay, Seine, Louvre, Tuileries

Résidence Latour Maubourg ★★
150, rue de Grenelle (7th)

15 rooms, 10 with bath or shower and toilet

I could move right into this charming pension-hotel, and, in fact, many people have done just that. One guest arrived more than 20 years ago and is still here. Others come for months at a time, and, over the years, several well-known authors have made this their Paris address.

Facing the Invalides across a small park, this town house has been in the Klein family for more than 150 years and was their home until they opened it to paying guests. In the transition, they have done a wonderful job of making guests feel welcome, offering all the amenities of a hotel while retaining the feeling of a fine home by keeping their museum-quality heirlooms in place.

The first floor has an enjoyable plant-filled salon with the family cat, Lulu, often lazily stretched across the sunniest spot on the carpet. A mahogany staircase leads up from the marble-floored foyer to the second- and third-floor bedrooms. Each is individually furnished with antiques from different periods, and almost all have nice full bathrooms. The accommodations range from a sunny single to a grand Louis XV double with a marble fireplace and two balconies overlooking the park in front. For a longer stay, the striking two-room suite with its second-floor loggia is always in great demand.

You may take all of your meals, or only breakfast, in the large dining room with its massive brass chandelier, working stone fireplace, and polished oak floors. The tables are set for every meal with crisp linens and quality china, stemware, and silver, so there is never a boardinghouse aura.

If this very special Parisian pension-hotel appeals

TELEPHONE
45-51-75-28

TELEX
None

FAX
None

MÉTRO
Latour-Maubourg

CREDIT CARDS
MC, V

RATES
Single 190–510F, double 420–655F, suite/apartment 620–765F

BREAKFAST
Continental breakfast 32F, lunch 95F, dinner 85F; wine extra

to you, make your plans as early as possible and secure your request with a deposit.

English Spoken: Yes

Facilities and Services: Direct-dial phones, TV in salon and in dining room

Nearest Tourist Attractions (Left Bank): Invalides, Rodin Museum, Musée d'Orsay, Seine

EIGHTH ARRONDISSEMENT

EIGHTH ARRONDISSEMENT
Right Bank: American Embassy, Arc de Triomphe and Étoile, Champs-Élysées, elegant shopping, Madeleine Church, Petit and Grand Palais, Place de la Concorde

The Champs-Élysées, sweeping dramatically from the Place de la Concorde to the Arc de Triomphe, is the most famous avenue in the world and definitely worth a serious stroll. But save the shopping, partying, and eating for less touristy and unspoiled areas. This is the traditional watering hole for show-biz celebrities, glamor girls, tourists in jogging shoes, heavy-set men and their young companions, and anyone else who wants to hide behind dark glasses. The flame on the tomb of the unknown soldier burns under the Arc de Triomphe, and the view from the top is just as inspiring. Twelve avenues radiate from the Arc, forming the world-famous, death-defying traffic circle known as the Étoile.

The Place de la Concorde is the largest square in Paris and one of the most strikingly beautiful anywhere in the world. It is thrilling to stand here day or night and be surrounded by some of the greatest landmarks in the world: the Tuileries Gardens; the Louvre; and the view up the Champs-Élysées to the Arc de Triomphe, across the Seine to the Palais Bourbon and up the Rue Royale to the Madeleine Church. In the evenings when it is all illuminated and the fountains are playing, it is a sight you will never forget.

HÔTELS IN THE EIGHTH ARRONDISSEMENT
Hôtel Bradford ★★★
Hôtel Concortel ★★★
Hôtel de l'Élysée ★★★
Hôtel du Ministére ★★
Hôtel Folkestone ★★★
Hôtel Lido ★★★

Hôtel Marigny ★★
Hôtel Mayflower ★★★
Hôtel Queen Mary ★★★
Résidence Lord Byron ★★★
Timhôtel Saint-Lazare ★★

Hôtel Bradford ★★★
10, rue St-Philippe-du-Roule (8th)
48 rooms, all with bath or shower and toilet

The Bradford offers peace and quiet only a five-minute stroll from the noise and crowds along the Champs-Élysées. Over the years, this graceful, old-style hotel has lost none of its charming appeal. From the moment guests enter the antiques-filled lobby and reception rooms, an attentive staff, headed by M. and Mme Mourot, is there to serve and make them feel right at home.

A wonderful turn-of-the-century wood and glass elevator lifts guests to the spacious, high-ceilinged bedrooms, many of which have marble fireplaces and floor-to-ceiling windows. All rooms are spotless, and pleasingly furnished with comfortable armchairs, dressers to encourage unpacking, and nice tables for postcard and letter writing. There is also plenty of closet space and luggage room, a rarity in most Parisian hotel rooms. The modern bathrooms, which come with monogrammed towels, bars of scented soap, and heated towel racks, have more space than you will ever use. There are several adjoining suites, and some of the larger rooms have small living rooms off the bedrooms, making them excellent choices for families.

English Spoken: Yes

Facilities and Services: Direct-dial phones, elevator, room service for light snacks, TVs for 50F per day

Nearest Tourist Attractions (Right Bank): Champs-Élysée, shopping along Rue Faubourg St-Honoré, Arc de Triomphe

TELEPHONE
43-59-24-20

TELEX
BRADFORD 648-530 F

FAX
None

MÉTRO
St-Philippe-du-Roule

CREDIT CARDS
MC, V

RATES
Single 605–660F, double 715–770F, triple 950F, suite/apartment 825F; extra bed 175F, baby crib 75F

BREAKFAST
Continental, 28F; included but can be deducted

Hôtel Concortel ★★★
21, rue Pasquier (8th)

TELEPHONE
42-65-45-44
TELEX
660-228 F
FAX
(1) 42-65-18-33
MÉTRO
St-Lazare, St-Augustin
CREDIT CARDS
AE, DC, MC, V
RATES
1 or 2 persons 550–600F,
suite/apartment 700F
BREAKFAST
Continental, 40F

46 rooms, all with bath or shower and toilet

Offering all the modern conveniences that appeal to repeat guests, the Concortel continues to improve each year and has my endorsement as a winning stopover in the center of Paris. A uniformed professional staff is always ready to provide polite service to help make a stay here worry-free and relaxing. There are two blocks of rooms joined by a lushly landscaped courtyard. The spacious rooms are all very well arranged, with tone-on-tone wallpaper, good-looking furniture, and impressive closet space. The real attractions for many, however, are the pink and beige marble bathrooms, some with double sinks and all with huge tubs and plenty of space. One even has its own closet, dressing table, and enough floor space to practice vigorous aerobics. Some of the best values in hotel suites can be found at the Concortel. All the suites are roomy and, for the price, are ideal for families or anyone needing more space for a longer stay.

English Spoken: Yes

Facilities and Services: Bar, direct-dial phones, elevator (in first building), mini-bars, porter, same-day laundry service (Mon–Sat), radios, TVs with international reception

Nearest Tourist Attractions (Right Bank): Place Vendôme, Madeleine Church, Concorde, old Opéra, Galeries Lafayette and Au Printemps department stores

Hôtel de l'Élysée ★★★
12, rue des Saussaies (8th)

TELEPHONE
42-65-29-25
TELEX
281-665 F
FAX
(1) 42-65-64-28
MÉTRO
Champs-Élysées Clemenceau,
Miromesnil
CREDIT CARDS
AE, DC, MC, V
RATES
Single 510–895F, double 580–
895F, suite 1,270F

32 rooms, all with bath or shower and toilet

The delightful Élysée sits in a very quiet and safe Right Bank location across from the Ministry of the Interior. It is also within walking distance to the Place de la Concorde, the Madeleine Church, the lower end of the Tuileries, and designer shopping on Rue Faubourg St-Honoré.

The rich downstairs salon is filled with period French furnishings and paintings. A splendid mirrored staircase with faux marble panels winds up to the well-lighted hallways. An elevator reaches all but the sixth floor, but the walk up the small flight of stairs is worth it for the quiet view suites, some with Napoleonic campaign beds and side curtains. The nicely appointed rooms on the other floors, the moderate prices for this expensive area, and excellent service all make this one of the best, if not *the* best value in the locality.

English Spoken: Yes

Facilities and Services: Bar, direct-dial phones, elevator to all but 6th-floor suites, hair dryers, mini-bars in suites, porter, TVs

Nearest Tourist Attractions (Right Bank): Concorde, Madeleine Church, designer boutiques on Rue Faubourg St-Honoré

Hôtel du Ministère ★★
31, rue de Surène (8th)
28 rooms, all with bath or shower and toilet

When asked to provide the names of two-star winners on the Right Bank near the American Embassy and the Champs-Élysées, the Hôtel du Ministère definitely tops my list. Just between us, it is the sort of hotel guidebook writers are tempted to keep to themselves or to share with only a few select friends. Now into its fourth generation of running the hotel, the Blanc family has finished refurbishing it with spectacular results, providing guests with every comfort and convenience.

It would be impossible to go far wrong in any of the perfectly tailored rooms, with their oak beams, attractive Italian lights, family antiques, beautiful baths, and coordinated color schemes and fabrics. In addition to the well-tended rooms, the reasonable prices and hospitable atmosphere combine to make this a very good choice that is recommended by all who stay here.

English Spoken: Yes

Facilities and Services: Direct-dial phones, elevator, hair dryers, mini-bars, radios, TVs with international reception

Nearest Tourist Attractions (Right Bank): Champs-Élysées, Place de la Concorde, shopping on Rue St-Honoré, Tuileries

BREAKFAST
Continental with fresh orange juice, 55F

TELEPHONE
42-66-21-43

TELEX
None

FAX
(1) 42-66-96-04

MÉTRO
Madeleine

CREDIT CARDS
AE, MC, V

RATES
Single 325–490F, double 490–600F

BREAKFAST
Continental, 35F

Hôtel Folkestone ★★★
9, rue Castellane (8th)
49 rooms, all with bath or shower and toilet

TELEPHONE
42-65-73-09; toll free from the U.S. and Canada: 800-528-1234

TELEX
290-431 F

FAX
(1) 42-65-64-09

MÉTRO
Madeleine, Havre-Caumartin

CREDIT CARDS
AE, DC, MC, V

RATES
Single 675–715F, double 715F, triple 865F, quad 950F

BREAKFAST
Buffet, 55F

The Folkestone is one of the brightest stars of the Best Western chain in Paris and definitely one of the better choices in an area where prices are usually *way* over the top. A stay here puts you in the middle of the business, high fashion, and entertainment precinct of the city.

The contemporary bedrooms are decorated in peach, pale gray, and cream, with grass-cloth-covered walls, marble baths, and, in most rooms, good closet space. The smallest doubles on the back are quiet but have miniature bathrooms and no view. The bright, cheerful rooms on the street have double window panes and good general space.

Breakfast is very special here. Every morning one of the maids, whose hobby is cooking, rises at dawn to prepare luscious *tartes*, cakes, quiches, and a fresh fruit compote. These are placed on the buffet breakfast table along with yogurt, boiled eggs, hot brioches, *pain au chocolate*, croissants, sweet butter, and assorted jams. English tea, American or French coffee, and hot chocolate are also served. For my money, this sumptous meal is reason enough to stay at the Folkestone.

English Spoken: Yes

Facilities and Services: Bar, direct-dial phones, elevator, mini-bars, room safes, TVs, videos, radios

Nearest Tourist Attractions (Right Bank): Madeleine Church, old Opéra, shopping on Rue Faubourg St-Honoré and at Au Printemps and Galeries Lafayette

Hôtel Lido ★★★
4, passage de la Madeleine (8th)
32 rooms, all with bath or shower and toilet

TELEPHONE
42-66-27-37; toll free in U.S. and Canada: 800-528-1234

TELEX
281-039 F LIDOTEL

FAX
(1) 42-66-61-23

For the ultimate center-city location, close to almost everything by foot or Métro, the Lido is a stellar choice. Bright red-geranium-filled window boxes set the hotel apart on the little *passage* off the Place de la Madeleine. An 18th-century Aubusson tapestry dominates the reception and lobby. Exposed beams, magnificent hand-rubbed antiques, and masses of fresh flowers complete the charming beginning. Even the smallest red-linen-lined rooms have enough living space. Mini-bars are hidden in heavy wooden furniture, and delicate lace spreads cover the large beds. Appreciated extras such as full-length mirrors, sewing kits, scented soaps, and personalized service make the Lido one of the top Best Western hotels in Paris.

English Spoken: Yes

Facilities and Services: Bar, direct-dial phones, elevator, hair dryers, mini-bars, room safes, clocks, radios, TVs with international reception

Nearest Tourist Attractions (Right Bank): Madeleine Church, Fauchon, Concorde, Louvre, Palais-Royal, old Opéra, shopping at Galeries Lafayette and Au Printemps, Champs-Élysées, Tuileries

MÉTRO
Madeleine

CREDIT CARDS
AE, DC, MC, V

RATES
Single 715F, double 820F, triple 925F, suite 820–1,303F

BREAKFAST
Buffet, 30F; included but can be deducted

Hôtel Marigny ★★
11, rue de l'Arcade (8th)

32 rooms, 26 with bath or shower and toilet; 6 very small rooms with shower, no toilet

Only a few hundred yards from the Madeleine Church and a bracing ten minutes from Gare St-Lazare and Place de la Concorde is this Cheap Sleep. The neighborhood is as dull as dishwater after 7 P.M. and on weekends, but the prices are right and the Métro is close. The hotel is a little faded here and there and generally in need of paint, new fabrics, and better carpeting, but if you are lucky and land in one of the improved rooms, you will probably love it. If you only need a clean place to shower and sleep, then any room will fill the bill. The rooms are reached by the same antique bird-cage elevator that Marcel Proust used when he lived and wrote in the hotel. Most of the rooms are sunny, several connect, and some on the top floor have balconies where you can step outside and enjoy the view.

English Spoken: Yes

Facilities and Services: Direct-dial phones, elevator, TVs and mini-bars in larger rooms

TELEPHONE
42-66-42-71, 42-66-42-74

TELEX
None

FAX
(1) 47-42-06-76

MÉTRO
Madeleine, Havre-Caumartin

CREDIT CARDS
MC, V

RATES
1 or 2 persons 200F (no toilet), 1 or 2 persons 400F (full facilities); extra bed 150F

BREAKFAST
Continental, 30F

Nearest Tourist Attractions (Right Bank): Madeleine Church, Tuileries, Place Vendôme, Concorde, old Opéra, shopping at Galeries Lafayette and Au Printemps

Hôtel Mayflower ★★★
3, rue Chateaubriand (8th)

24 rooms, all with bath or shower and toilet

TELEPHONE
42-62-57-46

TELEX
640-727 MAYFLOW

FAX
(1) 42-56-32-38

MÉTRO
George-V, Charles-de-Gaulle
Étoile

CREDIT CARDS
MC, V

RATES
Single 540–655F, double 655–810F; extra bed for children only, 130F

BREAKFAST
Continental, 45F

The Mayflower is a classically French hotel on a quiet side street close to the Champs-Élysées, and is part of a group of outstanding hotels owned and managed by the Benoit family (see Résidence Lord Byron, page 113).

The building dates back to Napoléon III, so all is not *au courant*. The rooms are generally an attractive mixture of reproduction furniture with easy chairs, small writing desks, good lighting, comfortable beds, roomy closets, and sizable bathrooms—some with double sinks. One of the nicest aspects of this hotel is the captivating garden with shade trees and lovely flowers. In the warmer months, breakfast is served here, and drinks in the afternoon and evening. The rest of the year, breakfast is served in a room designed to resemble a ship, with a sea mural along one wall and a curved wooden ceiling. In an area where it is difficult to find an acceptable room for less than $175 per night per person, the Mayflower outclasses its nearest rival and is one to count on.

English Spoken: Yes

Facilities and Services: Direct-dial phones, elevator, mini-bars, room safes, TVs with international reception

Nearest Tourist Attractions (Right Bank): Arc de Triomphe, Champs-Élysées, deluxe shopping on Avenues Marceau and George V

Hôtel Queen Mary ★★★
9, rue Greffulhe (8th)

36 rooms, all with bath or shower and toilet

TELEPHONE
42-66-40-50

TELEX
640-419 F

For visitors to Paris with champagne tastes but a Perrier budget, who desire a distinguished hotel in the heart of the city between the old Opéra and the

Madeleine Church, it is hard to do better than the Queen Mary. A cordial reception from owners M. and Mme Jaouen sets the welcoming tone. During the 35 years that they have owned this hotel, the Jaouens have provided peacefully livable accommodations to their many guests. Mme Jaouen is in charge of all the interiors, and she has done a masterful job. On the ground floor, there is a graceful lobby joined by two side salons with beautiful Louis XIV furniture. Towards the back is an inviting covered garden with a water fountain and tables for breakfast, a soft drink, or talking with other guests. The well-lighted halls lead to traditional rooms with large windows, elegant marble baths, and good closet space. The hotel undergoes a yearly upgrading and painting. On a daily basis, everything is kept clean by an armada of maids crisply dressed in black uniforms in the winter and seersucker in the summer, wearing little white caps and looking exactly like the perfect "French maid."

English Spoken: Yes

Facilities and Services: Direct-dial phones, elevator, hair dryers, TVs

Nearest Tourist Atrtractions (Right Bank): Madeleine Church, old Opéra, shopping at Galeries Lafayette and Au Printemps

FAX
(1) 42-66-94-92

MÉTRO
Madeleine, Havre-Caumartin

CREDIT CARDS
MC, V

RATES
Single 580–630F, double 630–730F; extra bed 100–150F

BREAKFAST
Continental, 45F

Résidence Lord Byron ★★★
5, rue Chateaubriand (8th)
30 rooms, all with bath or shower and toilet

The Résidence Lord Byron continues to provide excellence for half the price of many other hotels in this prestigious *quartier*. On a quiet, winding street less than five minutes from the bright lights and excitement of the Champs-Élysées, it is so peaceful that it is listed in the *European Guide to Silent Hotels*. The large, personalized rooms are elegantly comfortable, and are furnished with a wide range of antiques and reproductions. The colors are soft and pleasing, the accessories appropriate, and the fabrics well coordinated. Most of the 30 rooms overlook a garden courtyard where morning coffee is served in the summer. Because this fine hotel sets the standard to which

TELEPHONE
43-59-89-98

TELEX
649-662 F

FAX
(1) 42-89-46-04

MÉTRO
George-V

CREDIT CARDS
MC, V

RATES
Single 685F, double 735–842F, suite 1,135–1,300F; extra bed 165F

BREAKFAST
Continental, 50F

others aspire, it is easy to see why so many well-traveled guests make this their Paris pied-à-terre.

English Spoken: Yes

Facilities and Services: Bar, direct-dial phones, elevator, some hair dryers, mini-bars, room safes, TVs with international reception

Nearest Tourist Attractions (Right Bank): Arc de Triomphe, Champs-Élysées

Timhôtel Saint-Lazare ★★

TELEPHONE
43-87-53-53
TELEX
290-044 F
FAX
(1) 43-87-66-25
MÉTRO
St-Lazare
RATES
Single 415F, double 480–510F, triple 625F; sauna 45F
BREAKFAST
Continental in room, 48F; served downstairs, 35F

113, rue St-Lazare (8th)

See page 35 for general information on all the Timhôtels.

English Spoken: Yes

Facilities and Services: Bar, conference room, direct-dial phones, TVs, videos, radios, sauna

Nearest Tourist Attractions (Right Bank): *Grand boulevards*, Galeries Lafayette and Au Printemps department stores

NINTH ARRONDISSEMENT

NINTH ARRONDISSEMENT
Right Bank: *Grands boulevards, grands magazins* (Au Printemps and Galeries Lafayette), old Opéra, Pigalle

In the ninth arrondissement, one quickly appreciates the long-range influence of the brilliant urban planner Baron Haussmann when walking along the wide, tree-lined boulevards that lead to the Place de la République. At the northern end is the infamous Pigalle, a sleazy 24-hour neighborhood lined with peep shows, bordellos, "ladies of the night," and everything else you can imagine that walks on the seamy side of life.

HOTELS IN THE NINTH ARRONDISSEMENT
Hôtel des Arts ★★
Hôtel des Trois Poussins **no stars**

Hôtel des Arts ★★

7, Cité Bergère; entrance at 6, rue du Faubourg Montmartre (9th)

24 rooms, all with bath or shower and toilet

The Cité Bergère is a *passage* in central Paris that has eight hotels offering more than 400 rooms to weary travelers. The pretty pink and white flower-filled Hôtel des Arts is the best of the bunch by far. While it is nothing fancy, the prices appeal to couples on budgets who want a peaceful night's sleep in a busy city location. The rooms all display a wondrous mixture of period furniture, flocked and flowered wallpaper, chrome, plastic, fringe, ruffles, and chenille. The pretty glass dining room has a wagon filled with flowers and green plants. In one corner, Babar the colorful bird talks and whistles a happy tune. While hardly a tourist mecca, the location is within walking distance of the Folies Bergère and a Métro stop or two away from Montmartre. Motorists take note: The hotel has four free parking spaces. In any part of Paris, that convenience and savings alone is worth double the price of the room.

English Spoken: Yes

Facilities and Services: Bar, direct-dial phones, elevator to 4th floor only, TVs, 4 free parking spaces

Nearest Tourist Attractions (Right Bank): Folies Bergère, old Opéra, shopping at Galeries Lafayette and Au Printemps

TELEPHONE
42-46-73-30

TELEX
250-303 F; attention Hôtel des Arts

FAX
(1) 48-00-94-42

MÉTRO
Rue Montmartre; exit Faubourg Montmartre

CREDIT CARDS
AE, DC, MC, V

RATES
Single 320–345F, double 345–375F, triple 510F; extra bed 100F

BREAKFAST
Continental, 28F

Hôtel des Trois Poussins (no stars)
15, rue Clauzel (9th)

18 rooms, 10 with bath, shower, or toilet, to rent by the day or week; 25 rooms, none with toilet, some with shower, to rent by the month

In the part of Paris north of the *grands boulevards* and south of Pigalle, finding a Cheap Sleep is not very hard. The hard part is finding a decent one. Look no farther than the Trois Poussins, a remarkable no-star gem on Rue Clauzel. The rooms rent by the day, week, or month, and a few even include unequipped kitchens, an unheard-of extra at these giveaway prices. Okay, so some of the floors slope, a few spots are on the worn carpets, the decor is patchy, and one of the kitchens is in the corner of the bathroom. At these prices you expect more? Listed in many student and backpacker guides to Paris, reservations for the rooms

TELEPHONE
48-74-38-20

TELEX
None

FAX
None

MÉTRO
St-Georges

CREDIT CARDS
None; cash only

RATES
1 or 2 persons 130–230F (short terms), 1 or 2 persons 75–150F per day (monthly); hall shower 15F

BREAKFAST
Continental (no croissants), 20F

should be made months in advance and *must* be accompanied with a one-night deposit in French francs. The long-term accommodations have a months-long waiting list, and while management prefers to rent these to students or other non-tourists, they assured me that everyone's money is equal when reserving.

English Spoken: Not very much

Facilities and Services: Black and white TVs for rent

Nearest Tourist Attractions (Right Bank): Pigalle, Montmartre

TENTH, ELEVENTH, TWELFTH, AND THIRTEENTH ARRONDISSEMENTS

These arrondissements are known as the *quartier populaires* because they are traditionally working-class neighborhoods where many foreigners settle. With the exception of the emerging 11th around the Bastille, these are not hotbeds of tourist activity, but they do provide interesting glimpses of the blue-collar Parisian way of life.

The neighborhood around the Bastille is the city's new bohemia, full of art galleries, artists' lofts, cafés, night clubs, and new wave boutiques. It hums night and day and is definitely the "in" place to see and be seen.

HOTELS IN THE ELEVENTH ARRONDISSEMENT
Daval Hôtel ★★

Daval Hôtel ★★
21, rue Daval (11th)

23 rooms, all with bath or shower and toilet

TELEPHONE
47-00-51-23

TELEX
None

FAX
(1) 40-21-80-26

Valued mainly for its "in" location and price, the Daval Hôtel occupies a platinum position in the white-hot Bastille area, only a short promenade from the new Opéra and all the avant-garde cafés, bars, boutiques, and galleries that characterize this newly popular *quartier*.

All the rooms are done in the same basic, minimalistic style: open closets, compact baths, built-in beds and side tables, and no chairs or stools for seating. The walls are mercifully thick enough to buffer the neighbor's snoring or late-night television. You will find Hugo the German shepherd mascot stretched out across the floor in the all-purpose lobby and reception area where owner M. Gonod runs his little hotel with good sense, good humor, and kindness.

English Spoken: Yes

Facilities and Services: Direct-dial phones, elevator, hair dryers, TVs

Nearest Tourist Attractions (Right Bank): Bastille area, new Opéra

METRO
Bastille, Bréguet-Sabin

CREDIT CARDS
MC, V

RATES
Single 315F, double 370–475F, triple 475F, quad 580F

BREAKFAST
Continental, 40F

HOTELS IN THE THIRTEENTH ARRONDISSEMENT
Timhôtel Italie ★★

Timhôtel Italie ★★
22, rue Barrault (13th)

See page 35 for general information on all the Timhôtels.

English Spoken: Yes

Facilities and Services: Conference room, direct-dial phones, elevator, TVs, videos, radios

Nearest Tourist Attractions (Right Bank): Very far from tourist attractions. Close to Cité Universitaire, the huge institution of higher learning in Paris

TELEPHONE
45-80-67-67

TELEX
205-461 F

FAX
(1) 45-89-36-93

METRO
Corvisart

RATES
Single 288F, double 415–450F; extra bed 100F

BREAKFAST
Continental; 35F downstairs, 45F in room

FOURTEENTH ARRONDISSEMENT

In recent years, Montparnasse has become the victim of an insensitive redevelopment policy exemplified by the Tour Montparnasse. During the 1920s and 1930s, the 14th represented the Golden Age of

FOURTEENTH ARRONDISSEMENT
Left Bank: Montparnasse

Paris. It was well known as the artistic headquarters of the modern art and literary worlds. Nostalgia buffs return today and head for the historic brasseries Le Dôme and La Coupole to rekindle memories of the famous who ate and drank there, but they find that the spirit just isn't the same.

HOTELS IN THE FOURTEENTH ARRONDISSEMENT

Grand Hôtel du Square **no stars**
Hôtel Floridor ★
Hôtel Istria ★★
Hôtel l'Aiglon ★★★
Hôtel Novanox ★★★
Timhôtel le Maine ★★

Grand Hôtel du Square (no stars)
2, rue Boulard (14th)

TELEPHONE
43-22-50-09

TELEX
None

FAX
None

MÉTRO
Denfert-Rochereau

CREDIT CARDS
None; cash only

RATES
Single 100–140F, double 155F; hall shower 10F

BREAKFAST
Not served

30 rooms, none with bath or shower or toilet

The Grand Hôtel du Square is certainly *not* grand—in fact it hasn't had a face lift in years, but then neither have the rates, which can be described as almost prehistoric. In addition, its location far from the excitement and bright lights isn't what I would call thrilling. But—for Cheap Sleepers who find adventure in off-beat, low-budget digs, this could be the right hotel. The bare-bones rooms are done in the attic school of decorating, without carpets or bedside lamps—only an overhead light of questionable wattage. Some rooms have ornate marble fireplaces; others display lovely old armoires. All rooms are spacious and clean as a whistle. Each floor has a toilet, and there are three showers in the hotel—all of which are clean enough that you can leave the Lysol in the suitcase. There is no breakfast served, and no one makes any attempt to speak English, unless you happen to run into the owner's daughter who stops by now and then to visit her mother. The Métro stop isn't far and bus connections are good.

English Spoken: No
Facilities and Services: None. *Important*: Hotel

locks front door at midnight and does not provide keys, so guests must be in before "curfew."

Nearest Tourist Attractions (Left Bank): Nothing; must use public transportation

Hôtel Floridor ★
28, place Denfert-Rochereau (14th)
50 rooms, 44 with bath or shower and toilet

The Floridor is a Cheap Sleeps find just off the Place Denfert Rochereau. You will be away from the tourist crowds in this neighborhood, which is near Montparnasse and interesting in its own right because of its blue-collar simplicity. The guests at the hotel are an international set of students, artists, and intellectuals on shoestring budgets who travel smart by sleeping cheap.

The large second-floor hotel is old-fashioned compared to the trendy renovated ones that dot St-Germain-des-Prés and most of the Marais, but it is appealing nonetheless in a homey sort of way. The price of the room naturally depends on its size and the specifics of its plumbing, but everything is always kept scrupulously clean and freshly painted, papered, and polished. M. Narcy, the manager for almost 25 years, speaks no English but makes up for it in good will and patience with those who must resort to rusty high-school French phrases.

English Spoken: No

Facilities and Services: Direct-dial phones, elevator, TVs

Nearest Tourist Attractions (Left Bank): Nothing within easy walking distance, but Métro is close and so is excellent bus service

TELEPHONE
43-21-35-53

TELEX
None

FAX
(1) 43-27-65-81

MÉTRO
Denfert-Rochereau

CREDIT CARDS
None; cash only

RATES
Single 340–380F, double 260–305F

BREAKFAST
Continental with croissants, included; cannot be deducted

Hôtel Istria ★★
29, rue Campagne Première (14th)
26 rooms, all with bath or shower and toilet

From this address you can wander the tree-lined boulevards and sit in the famous cafés that were the watering holes of Hemingway, Fitzgerald, and Henry Miller when they dominated the Montparnasse literary scene. In the twenties and thirties, when this was

TELEPHONE
43-20-91-82

TELEX
203-618 F

FAX
(1) 43-22-48-45

MÉTRO
Raspail

CREDIT CARDS
MC, V

RATES
Single 440F, double 490–540F;
extra bed 120F

BREAKFAST
Continental, 40F

the quartier for artists and writers, the Istria was home to many of them, including Man Ray and his mistress Kiki, Marcel Duchamp, and the poet Maiakowsky. Now, under the direction of Philippe Leroux and his charming wife Danièle, the hotel has been totally renovated and has become a favorite for those seeking a convenient Montparnasse location. A pretty tiled entry with country antiques and Oriental rugs leads to a postage-stamp garden along the back of the hotel. Some of the rooms that overlook the garden are confining for two persons with any luggage. To avoid being cramped, request a third-floor nest. Remember though, this building is old, and spacious rooms are not its strong suit, but charm and friendliness are.

English Spoken: Yes

Facilities and Services: Direct-dial phones, elevator, hair dryers, room safes, TVs, radios

Nearest Tourist Attractions (Left Bank): Montparnasse

Hôtel l'Aiglon ★★★
232, boulevard Raspail (14th)
47 rooms, all with bath or shower and toilet

TELEPHONE
43-20-82-42

TELEX
206-038 F

FAX
(1) 43-20-98-72

MÉTRO
Raspail

CREDIT CARDS
AE, DC, MC, V

RATES
Single 445F, double 505–660F, suites 930–1,400F; extra bed 100F, parking 75F per day

BREAKFAST
Continental, 35F

The Aiglôn is a refined hotel about a one-minute walk from the Raspail Métro stop. The formal decor is carried throughout the downstairs, from the faux-book-lined bar to the old-fashioned breakfast room with its round mahogany tables covered in starched white linens. When reserving, *insist* on a remodeled room or suite, and you will be content. Otherwise, the unmodernized rooms are racing toward the 1950s in a frumpy manner and should be avoided at all costs. The newer rooms have all been planned with discretion and good taste. They have color-coordinated textured fabrics, firm mattresses, good closet and luggage space, and the latest in bathrooms. The new suites are dreams come true, especially No. 59 with its separate sitting room, a double-sink bathroom, and a balcony with peaceful views over the famous *Cimetière* Montparnasse. Motorists will appreciate the private parking available when reserving a room, and everyone will enjoy the welcome provided by Jacques Rols (who also owns Le Notre Dame Hôtel, page 65) and his helpful staff.

English Spoken: Yes

Facilities and Services: Bar, direct-dial phones, elevator, hair dryers, mini-bars, parking (75F per day), TVs with international reception

Nearest Tourist Attractions (Left Bank): Montparnasse

Hôtel Novanox ★★★
155, boulevard du Montparnasse (14th)
27 rooms, all with bath or shower and toilet

From the outside it looks like almost any other three-star hotel. But inside, the future beckons. What used to be the Hôtel de Nice, a basic budget hotel in Montparnasse, is now the dazzling Novanox, a textbook example of what a sense of style and a great imagination—with a little money thrown in—can do with an old hotel. Hats off to owner Bernard Plasmans, who gambled everything on creating a modern fantasy hotel that displays the latest in hotel design and contemporary craftsmanship. The yellow and blue lobby, with dangling mobile lights and faces of Greek gods and goddesses softly painted on the walls and depicted on the upholstered chairs and couches, reminds me of a playful fairyland. At one end of the main floor, the breakfast area looks out onto the passing parade from behind floor-to-ceiling picture windows. Dainty croissants, *petits pains aux raisins*, and buttery brioches fill the breakfast baskets and are accompanied with an assortment of jams and a pot of sweet butter.

Upstairs the rooms have a perfectly coordinated pastel color scheme, with contemporary furniture especially created to fit the specifics of each room. The lamps are from Spain, the thick carpet imported from Germany, and the ideas are all M. Plasmans'. The result of it all? *Magnifique!*

English Spoken: Yes

Facilities and Services: Bar, direct-dial phones, elevator, mini-bars, TVs

Nearest Tourist Attractions (Left Bank): Montparnasse

TELEPHONE
46-33-63-60

TELEX
201-255 F

FAX
(1) 43-26-61-72

MÉTRO
Vavin, Raspail

CREDIT CARDS
AE, DC, MC, V

RATES
1 or 2 persons 650F; extra bed 150F

BREAKFAST
Continental, 40F

Timhôtel le Maine ★★
146, avenue du Maine (14th)

TELEPHONE
43-35-57-60
TELEX
205-036 F
FAX
(1) 40-47-01-49
MÉTRO
Gaîté
RATES
Single 350F, double 400–
450F; extra bed 100F
BREAKFAST
Continental; 45F in room,
35F downstairs

See page 35 for general information on all the Timhôtels.

English Spoken: Yes

Facilities and Services: Conference room, direct-dial phones, elevators, rooms for the handicapped, sauna, TVs, videos, radios

Nearest Tourist Attractions: None

FIFTEENTH ARRONDISSEMENT

FIFTEENTH ARRONDISSEMENT
Left Bank: La Tour
Montparnasse, UNESCO

The fifteenth, on the southwestern side of the city, has few tourist attractions and is basically a middle-class residential area.

HOTELS IN THE FIFTEENTH ARRONDISSEMENT
Hôtel Arès ★★
Hôtel Charles Quinze ★★
Hôtel Frantour-Suffren ★★★
Hôtel le Fondary ★★
3 Ducks Hostel ("Richies") **no stars**
Timhôtel Montparnasse ★★

Hôtel Arès ★★
7, rue du Général-de-Larminat (15th)
43 rooms, all with bath or shower and toilet

TELEPHONE
47-34-74-04
TELEX
206-083 F
FAX
(1) 47-34-48-56
MÉTRO
Motte-Picquet
CREDIT CARDS
AE, DC, MC, V
RATES
Single 440F, double 470F,
triple 600F, quad 650F
BREAKFAST
Continental, 35F

The Arès is a smart Cheap Sleep choice on a quiet street in a neighborhood of unqualified respectability. For high-scale shopping and dreaming, the Village Suisse antiques showrooms and shops are just around the corner. Or, for dreaming of another kind, in less than ten minutes you can be sitting in the Champ-de-Mars Park admiring the Eiffel Tower.

The public rooms are all attractive, especially the breakfast area, which is set off by a window garden filled with brightly blooming plants. Once you get beyond the dubious color schemes in the rooms, you will find them sparkling clean and providing all the conventional comforts at very reasonable rates. The walls in some of the rooms are thin, but, fortunately, the hotel is geared to a sedately middle-aged crowd that does not play loud radios or engage in midnight romps. The best rooms face front. My favorite is No. 15, a large corner room with two big windows and a nicely tiled bathroom.

English Spoken: Yes, and Italian and Spanish

Facilities and Services: Direct-dial phones, elevator, hair dryers, room safes, TVs with international reception

Nearest Tourist Attractions (Left Bank): Village Suisse, Champ-de-Mars, Eiffel Tower

Hôtel Charles Quinze ★★
37, rue St-Charles, corner of 36, rue Rouelle (15th)
30 rooms, all with bath or shower and toilet

The Charles XV might be considered by some to be in a tourist backwater. For others, it represents a change of pace, and is a safe bet for those insisting on peace in noisy Paris. I like it not only because it is well executed, but because it offers a glimpse of everyday life that you don't always see in the more congested *quartiers*. As you walk by the Place St-Charles, you will see old men quietly sitting under the shade of the chestnut trees reading their newspapers and talking about old times. Pretty young girls with long ribbons and smocked dresses rollerskate along the sidewalks, and women carrying brimming shopping baskets hurry from shop to shop picking just the right ingredients for their evening meal. For trips away from the hotel, a good Métro line is only a ten-minute walk and the Eiffel Tower about 20 if you window-shop along the route.

The hotel is done simply, but with great style. Blue and white Chinese porcelain creates an Oriental theme in the small whitewashed lobby. Each floor is coordinated in a different color. The rooms have country-style built-in furniture with matching draperies and bedspreads.

English Spoken: Yes

Facilities and Services: Direct-dial phones, eleva-

TELEPHONE
45-79-64-15

TELEX
202-005 F

FAX
(1) 45-77-21-11

MÉTRO
Charles-Michels, Dupleix

CREDIT CARDS
AE, DC, MC, V

RATES
Single 360F, double 400–480F; extra bed 120F

BREAKFAST
Continental (with cereal, cheese, juice, and yogurt), 40F

tor, hair dryers, mini-bars, TVs with international reception

Nearest Tourist Attractions (Left Bank): Not much; a 20 minutes' walk from Eiffel Tower.

Hôtel Frantour-Suffren ★★★
20, rue Jean Rey (15th)

417 rooms, all with bath or shower and toilet

TELEPHONE
45-78-61-08
TELEX
204-459 F
FAX
(1) 45-78-61-08
MÉTRO
Bir-Haikeim
CREDIT CARDS
AE, DC, MC, V
RATES
Single 815–1,089F, double 890–1,089F, apartment 2,090F; extra bed 200F, children under 12 free if they occupy their parent's room
BREAKFAST
Full American breakfast, 65F

Featuring mauve and pink bedrooms and suites with air-conditioning and free parking—two rarities in this price range—the Frantour-Suffren is one of the five Frantour hotels in Paris and the best of the lot by far. Possessing all the zip of an Elks Club and almost devoid of French zest, it is reminiscent of any large downtown hotel found in most major U.S. cities. Next door to the Hilton and in the shadow of the Eiffel Tower, it is a good choice for business travelers, groups, or those desiring every possible convenience.

The rooms are spacious and include excellent closet and shelf space, large desks, and big bathrooms. The choicest rooms are on the top two or three floors facing the Eiffel Tower. Here you can almost reach out and touch the moon as it floats by the Tower.

Be sure to avoid the mediocre (and high-priced) food in the hotel dining room and go instead to one of the nearby well-priced and interesting small restaurants listed in *Cheap Eats in Paris*.

English Spoken: Yes

Facilities and Services: Air-conditioning, bar, conference room, direct-dial phones, mini-bars, TVs with international reception, radios, clocks, rooms for handicapped, restaurant, duty-free shop, free parking, porters

Nearest Tourist Attractions (Left Bank): Eiffel Tower, Champ-de-Mars, Seine, Trocadéro

Hôtel le Fondary ★★
30, rue Fondary (15th)

20 rooms, all with bath or shower and toilet

TELEPHONE
45-75-14-75
TELEX
206-761 F

If you don't require much space and won't rebel at a blue-collar location in a tourist desert, then the Fondary is a quiet budget choice. Were it in a more tourist-inspired setting, it would command higher prices and probably be full all the time. The surrounding neighborhood provides a glimpse into Parisian bourgeois life that can be interesting, especially on your third or fourth trip when you want to see more of the "real" Paris. On Sundays, there is an enormous outdoor *marché* along Boulevard de Grenelle, and every day along Rue du Commerce you can watch daily life as shoppers crowd the stores and the open stalls that sell everything from housedresses, lampshades, and books to food, fresh flowers, and car parts. The hotel is actually much better than outward appearances would suggest. On the main floor, there is a pretty terrace off the dining room and a bar serving soft drinks and beer by the reception desk. Upstairs, the rooms are decorated in white bamboo with pastels and pretty fabrics. Prices match the size of the hotel: small.

English Spoken: Some

Facilities and Services: Bar (soft drinks, beer), direct-dial phones, elevator, mini-bars, TV with international reception

Nearest Tourist Attractions (Left Bank): Interesting blue-collar neighborhood; 25-minute walk to Eiffel Tower, must use Métro to anything else

FAX
(1) 45-75-84-42

MÉTRO
Émile-Zola, Motte-Picquet-Grenelle

CREDIT CARDS
AE, DC, MC, V

RATES
1 or 2 persons 390–430F

BREAKFAST
Continental, 40F

3 Ducks Hostel ("Richies") (no stars)
6, place Étienne Pernet (15th) (to right side of Jean Baptiste de Grenelle church at end of Rue du Commerce)

80 beds, 2 to 6 beds per room; 6 rooms have showers only, all others are without shower, bath, or toilet

One of the Cheapest Sleeps in Paris is found at the rugged 3 Ducks Hostel, better known to those in the know as "Richies—A Safe and Fun Place for You to Stay." This youthful hangout appeals to backpackers and other wanderers who value camaraderie along with wild and raucous fun over aesthetics or a peaceful night's rest. This is the sort of place where you must bring your own sheets and towels, or pay 10 francs rental the first night. The laid-back manage-

TELEPHONE
48-42-04-05

TELEX
None

FAX
None

MÉTRO
Commerce

CREDIT CARDS
None; cash only

RATES
75F per person per night, 450F per person per week

BREAKFAST
Not served

ment requires shirts and shoes to be worn at all times and provides cooking facilities, hot showers, summer barbecues, a TV lounge, and rooms for two, three, or four persons. There are no lockers, nor is there a minimum or maximum stay.

Guests must remember that cash is king when paying the bill, and they probably should not send their parents by to check the place out first.

English Spoken: Yes

Facilities and Services: Bar with beer and soft drinks

Nearest Tourist Attractions (Left Bank): Far from everything; must use public transportation

Timhôtel Montparnasse ★★
22, rue de l'Arrivée (15th)

TELEPHONE
45-48-96-62
TELEX
270-625 F
FAX
(1) 45-48-77-30
MÉTRO
Montparnasse-Bienvenue
RATES
Single 350F, double 400–450F; extra bed 100F
BREAKFAST
Continental; 35F downstairs, 45F in room

See page 35 for general information on all the Timhôtels.

English Spoken: Yes

Facilities and Services: Direct-dial phones, elevator, TVs, videos, radios

Nearest Tourist Attractions (Left Bank): Montparnasse

SIXTEENTH ARRONDISSEMENT

SIXTEENTH ARRONDISSEMENT
Right Bank: Avenue Foch, Bois de Boulogne, Jardin d'Acclimitation, Marmottan Museum, Passy, Trocadéro, shopping along Boulevard Victor-Hugo

Known as the home of the BCBG crowd (French yuppies), this is a quietly elegant neighborhood bordered by the Bois de Boulogne and the river Seine. Here you will see luxurious apartments on the Avenue Foch and engage in top-of-the-line shopping in Passy and along the Boulevard Victor Hugo. Trocadéro, directly across the Seine from the Eiffel Tower, is the name of the gardens around the Palais de Chaillot, an imposing two-winged building housing four museums. The spectacular view at night from the steps of Trocadéro across the Seine to the Eiffel Tower, with the illuminated pools, fountains, and statues between, is one you will never forget.

HOTELS IN THE SIXTEENTH ARRONDISSEMENT

Hôtel Ambassade ★★
Hôtel de Passy Eiffel ★★★
Hôtel de Sévigné ★★★
Hôtel du Bois ★★
Hôtel du Rond-Point de Longchamp ★★★
Hôtel Étoile-Maillot ★★★
Hôtel Frémiet ★★★
Hôtel Gavarni ★★
Hôtel Keppler ★★
Hôtel Massenet ★★★
Hôtel Nicolo ★★
Hôtel Regina de Passy ★★★
Hôtel Victor Hugo ★★★
Le Hameau de Passy ★★
Résidence Chambellan Morgane ★★★

Hôtel Ambassade ★★
79, rue Lauriston (16th)
38 rooms, all with bath or shower and toilet

For a practical stopover near the Étoile and Avenue Victor-Hugo, the Ambassade makes sense. The hotel is owned by the Mullie family (see Hôtel Victor Hugo, page 135), who maintain this two-star as a simple, friendly establishment that provides moderate rates to its loyal following. The rooms vary in size from small to medium and are equipped with lacquered wicker furniture, floral print wallpaper, and gray marble bathrooms. Those rooms on the ground floor have windows that open directly onto the street, creating a potential security problem, especially at night, so be sure to reserve a room on a higher floor.

English Spoken: Yes

Facilities and Services: Direct-dial phones, elevator, hair dryers, TVs

Nearest Tourist Attractions (Right Bank): Shopping on Avenue Victor-Hugo, Trocadéro

TELEPHONE
45-53-41-15, 54-53-28-26 for reservations

TELEX
613-643 F

FAX
(1) 45-53-69-93

MÉTRO
Boissière

CREDIT CARDS
MC, V

RATES
Single 435–490F, double 530–565F

BREAKFAST
Continental, 40F

Hôtel de Passy Eiffel ★★★
10, rue de Passy (16th)
50 rooms, all with bath or shower and toilet

TELEPHONE
45-25-55-26
TELEX
612-753 F
FAX
(1) 42-88-89-88
MÉTRO
Passy
CREDIT CARDS
AE, DC, MC, V
RATES
Single 575–590F, double 580–
615F, triple 680F
BREAKFAST
Continental, 35F

The Hôtel de Passy Eiffel continues to reflect high standards of excellence and gracious service. On the main street in Passy, it provides a first-hand look at one of Paris's most exclusive neighborhoods and some of the best shopping to be found. The marbled foyer and lobby face onto a garden courtyard with several rooms overlooking it. Two salons are tucked along each side, one with a grand piano and inviting seating, the other with a light and airy glassed-in garden breakfast room. A nice variety of rooms offer generous space and extra comfort. All have unusually pleasing views. From the top floor on the street side, guests can watch the elevator scale the Eiffel Tower as it takes tourists to various levels.

English Spoken: Yes

Facilities and Services: Bar, direct-dial phones, elevator, hair dryers, mini-bars, TVs with international reception

Nearest Tourist Attractions (Right Bank): Passy, Trocadéro

Hôtel de Sévigné ★★★
6, rue de Belloy (16th)

30 rooms, all with bath or shower and toilet

TELEPHONE
47-20-88-90
TELEX
610-219 F
FAX
(1) 40-70-98-73
MÉTRO
Boissière
CREDIT CARDS
AE, DC, MC, V
RATES
1 or 2 persons 610–710F;
parking at hotel 70F (*Note:*
Lower room rates from
July 21–August 31 and
December 21–January 6)
BREAKFAST
Continental, 45F

For value and location close to the Champs-Élysées, this dignified hotel provides all the conveniences most American travelers want. Facing the enchanting, tree-shaded Place des États-Unis, the hotel takes its name from Mme Sévigné, who was one of the foremost chroniclers of Parisian domestic life in the 1600s.

What the rooms may lack in style and imagination they more than make up for in size and cleanliness. Especially recommended for families are the large rooms and the doubles that can be connected to create suites. Another bonus if children are along is the hotel restaurant, which serves lunch and dinner during weekdays. The outstanding service provided by the pleasant desk staff adds to the benefits of this nice hotel.

English Spoken: Yes

Facilities and Services: Direct-dial phones, eleva-

tor, hair dryers, mini-bars, 3 hotel parking spaces (must be reserved in advance), room safes, radios, TVs with international reception

Nearest Tourist Attractions (Right Bank): Champs-Élysées, Arc de Triomphe, shopping on Avenue Victor-Hugo

Hôtel du Bois ★★
11, rue du Dome, corner of 29, avenue Victor-Hugo (16th)

41 rooms, all with bath or shower and toilet

For a stay on the exclusive Avenue Victor-Hugo with all its lovely shops, consider the Hôtel du Bois, a plain, friendly establishment that has no airs, but does boast a dedicated clientele who enjoy being only a few minutes from the Champs-Élysées. The entrance to the hotel is in a passageway reached on foot by steep steps from the street level, or by car on an upper level through one-way streets from behind. You will recognize the hotel by the pretty planter boxes under each window. The management continues to shine and polish the entire place, refurbishing the tired rooms and redoing the older bathrooms. They also provide a great deal of useful information—in English—on everything, from what to see and do to where to eat and to cash a check in the neighborhood. Rates are low for the area.

English Spoken: Yes

Facilities and Services: Direct-dial phones, mini-bars, TVs, free videos

Nearest Tourist Attractions (Right Bank): Champs-Élysées, Arc de Triomphe, shopping on Avenue Victor-Hugo and Avenue Marceau

TELEPHONE
45-00-31-96

TELEX
615-453 F

FAX
(1) 45-00-90-05

MÉTRO
Charles-de-Gaulle Étoile, Kléber

CREDIT CARDS
AE, MC, V

RATES
Single 410F, double 490F; extra bed 120F

BREAKFAST
Continental, 45F

Hôtel du Rond-Point de Longchamp ★★★
86, rue de Longchamp (16th)

57 rooms, all with bath or shower and toilet

The prevailing mood at the Rond-Point de Longchamp in the prestigious neighborhood between the Arc de Triomphe and La Tour Eiffel will appeal to

TELEPHONE
45-05-13-63

TELEX
OTELONG 640-883 F

FAX
(1) 47-55-12-80

MÉTRO
Trocadéro

CREDIT CARDS
AE, DC, MC, V

RATES
Single 620–775F, double 675–850F (ask about low-season rates)

BREAKFAST
Continental, 45F

traditionalists looking for exceptional value, classic heel-clicking service, and a multitude of facilities. The ground floor consists of a smart, plant-filled lounge, a bar, and a billiards room with soft leather armchairs. Some of the 57 rooms are decidedly Louis XIV, with four-poster beds and heavy curtains. Others reflect a more modern taste. Several are superbly planned for businesspeople. These rooms double as an office and sitting room during the day and have a comfortable pull-down bed for the night. All rooms have international-cable television reception, air-conditioning, and fabulous marble baths with every convenience you can imagine, including magnified shaving mirrors for men and scales to tell women if that last chocolate éclair is showing. The owner of this wonderful hotel, Gerard Dumontant, is the president of the independent hoteliers in France, so his hotel should reflect only the best, and let me assure you it does.

English Spoken: Yes

Facilities and Services: Air-conditioned rooms, bar, conference room, business services, direct-dial phones, elevator, TVs with international reception

Nearest Tourist Attractions (Right Bank): Trocadéro, shopping on Avenue Victor-Hugo

Hôtel Étoile-Maillot ★★★
10, rue du Bois de Boulogne, corner of rue Duret (16th)

26 rooms, all with bath or shower and toilet

TELEPHONE
45-00-42-60

TELEX
613-936 F

FAX
(1) 45-00-55-89

MÉTRO
Argentine, Charles-de-Gaulle Étoile

CREDIT CARDS
AE, MC, V

RATES
Single 540–665F, double 580–710F, suite 830F (1 person), suite 875F (2 persons); extra bed 170F

For elegant living in Paris, it is difficult to find higher quality than this hotel for the price. Although it is a bit far from the center of things on foot, the nearest Métro is a direct line to the Champs-Élysées, the Place de la Concorde, the Louvre, and the Bastille.

The Étoile-Maillot is a haven of comfort and tranquility on a shady street in the fashionable district around Avenue Foch and the Bois de Boulogne. The mood is like that of an elegant French home, the rooms beautifully furnished with an impressive collection of genuine Louis XV and XVI antiques, tapestry-covered chairs, Oriental rugs, silk wall coverings, and inlaid chests. The suite consisting of a sitting room, a bedroom with a king-size bed, and a lovely marble bath is wonderful for anyone who wants to work and entertain in a hotel room setting. The management's efforts show on a daily basis, from the bouquets of fresh flowers in the lobby to the white-glove cleanliness of the hotel in general. As a result, the Étoile-Maillot is a favorite and strongly recommended hotel.

English Spoken: Yes

Facilities and Services: Direct-dial phones, elevator, hair dryers, mini-bars, TVs

Nearest Tourist Attractions (Right Bank): Bois de Boulogne, Arc de Triomphe, Champs-Élysées, Palais des Congrès and Porte Maillot convention and exhibition centers

BREAKFAST
Continental, served in room; cannot be deducted

Hôtel Frémiet ★★★
6, avenue Frémiet (16th)

36 rooms, all with bath or shower and toilet

The Frémiet is in a neighborhood that was designed and built by Emmanuel Frémiet, a noted architect who has many of his sculptures on display at the Musée d'Orsay. Quietly positioned off Avenue du President Kennedy, this large hotel has been owned and run for almost 30 years by Claude Fourmond, who is also the president of the Best Western chain in France. This fact alone assures you that his own hotel will be among the best. From the pleasant lobby with its polite and eager desk staff headed by M. Mitri, to the seventh-story singles nested under the eaves, everything sails along in good order and is done in unobtrusive taste.

It is not within easy walking distance of much, but the No. 72 bus, which follows the river and passes all the major monuments and sites, stops a half block away, and the Passy Métro stop is only a five-minute walk. Motorists driving into Paris can get off the *périphérique* at Porte St-Cloud and be at the hotel door in under ten minutes without suffering the trauma of crossing town in wild traffic. Public parking is nearby. Another plus: Reservations can be made from the United States and Canada by calling a toll-free 800 number.

TELEPHONE
45-24-52-06; toll free from U.S. and Canada: 800-528-1234

TELEX
630-329 F

FAX
(1) 42-88-77-46

MÉTRO
Passy

CREDIT CARDS
AE, DC, MC, V

RATES
Single 550–800F, double 680–850F, suite 740–1,590F; extra bed 160F, free cribs and children under 12 free in parents' room

BREAKFAST
Continental; included but can be deducted

English Spoken: Yes

Facilities and Services: Air-conditioning in 10 rooms, direct-dial phones, elevator, hair dryers, minibars, TVs, radios

Nearest Tourist Attractions (Right Bank): Seine, Passy

Hôtel Gavarni ★★
5, rue Gavarni (16th)
30 rooms, all with bath or shower and toilet

TELEPHONE
45-24-52-82

TELEX
GAVARNI 612-338 F

FAX
(1) 40-50-16-95

MÉTRO
Passy

CREDIT CARDS
AE, DC, MC, V

RATES
Single 375–485F, double 520–540F

BREAKFAST
Continental, 35F

Hôtel Gavarni is an attractive choice on a quiet street in the center of Passy, one of Paris's most sought-after residential and shopping neighborhoods. It is owned and expertly run by the Mornands, whose backgrounds include extensive hotel experience in both France and the United States. They are a friendly couple who go out of their way to welcome American guests and take a personal interest in their needs.

Both the breakfast room and lobby are smartly done, with cane furniture and bright floral murals. Upstairs the rooms are small, but the furniture is pleasing and the beds very good. The bathrooms have folding doors to allow for more space, but are otherwise nicely appointed. Everything is always kept in top shape and is sparkling clean. The cozy singles on the back side of the hotel have corner marble fireplaces and are popular with many repeat visitors. Room No. 603 is another favorite because it has a view from both windows of the Eiffel Tower lighted at night.

English Spoken: Yes

Facilities and Services: Direct-dial phones, elevator, TVs with international reception

Nearest Tourist Attractions (Right Bank): Passy, Trocadéro

Hôtel Keppler ★★
12, rue Keppler (16th)
49 rooms, all with bath or shower and toilet

TELEPHONE
47-20-65-05

TELEX
640-544 F

FAX
(1) 47-23-02-29

For a two-star hotel, the Keppler offers much more than just a Cheap Sleep in a quiet location. It has, for one thing, honest-to-goodness room service, an unheard-of feature in almost all three-star hotels in Paris, let alone a two-star. For travelers with children, this can be a lifesaver in the evening.

For the prices, you can't expect luxury with deep-pile carpeting. The big rooms are efficiently ordinary, with sturdy Swedish-style desks and chairs and ample closet and drawer space. A team of uniformed maids wearing beepers keeps everything shipshape, and management keeps a lid on loud noises. There are many repeat guests, as well as some who stay for months at a time. It is easy to understand their enthusiasm for this hidden Parisian value, where reservations and a deposit are required far, far in advance of a stay.

English Spoken: Yes

Facilities and Services: Bar, elevator, direct-dial phones, TVs, room service for light snacks 9 A.M.– 7 P.M. daily

Nearest Tourist Attractions (Right Bank): Arc de Triomphe, Champs-Élysées, Guimet Museum, shopping on Avenue Victor-Hugo

MÉTRO
George V

CREDIT CARDS
AE, MC, V

RATES
1 or 2 persons 375–395F, 3 persons 482F

BREAKFAST
Continental, 30F

Hôtel Massenet ★★★
5 bis, rue Massenet (16th)
41 rooms, all with bath or shower and toilet

For a beautiful stay in Paris on a tranquil street in Passy, I like the formal Massenet. It is part of the Best Western group in Paris, so it must meet certain standards, and, in most cases, it exceeds them. The well-heeled French-executive clientele appreciates the quiet neighborhood close to the bon ton Passy shopping district, the professional services of the uniformed hotel staff, and, above all, the prices. These travelers know that if the Massenet were in a more mainstream location, the prices would be nearly doubled.

Downstairs, the public rooms are paneled in rich walnut. Soft seating, and a small library along one wall, create an appealing English intimacy. Morning croissants are served in a little alcove overlooking a colorful patio. All the rooms are well furnished and impeccably maintained. No. 70 has its own balcony and a walk-in closet that is almost as large as some hotel rooms I have seen. If traveling alone, request No. 71, a top-floor single with a view terrace.

TELEPHONE
45-24-43-03; toll free from U.S. and Canada: 800-528-1234

TELEX
640-196 F

FAX
(1) 45-24-41-39

MÉTRO
Passy

CREDIT CARDS
AE, DC, MC, V

RATES
Low- and high-season prices: Single 575–685F, double 655–765F; extra bed 175F

BREAKFAST
Continental, 35F

English Spoken: Yes

Facilities and Services: Direct-dial phones, elevator, hair dryers, some mini-bars, TVs

Nearest Tourist Attractions (Right Bank): Passy, Seine, Trocadéro

Hôtel Nicolo ★★
3, rue Nicolo (16th)

TELEPHONE
42-88-83-40

TELEX
649-585 F

FAX
(1) 42-24-45-41

MÉTRO
Passy, La Muette

CREDIT CARDS
MC, V

RATES
Single 350F, double 410–430F, triple 495F, quad 550F

BREAKFAST
Continental, included; cannot be deducted

28 rooms, all with bath or shower and toilet

Join diplomats visiting their nearby embassies, delegates to OECD, and other savvy travelers anxious to maximize their daily travel allowances by staying at the Nicolo in the center of Passy. What you save here you can spend engaging in guilt-free shopping at the designer discount shops on Rue de la Tour (see "Cheap Chic," page 163) or on Rue de Passy, one of Paris's premier shopping meccas for traditional, well-made clothing.

True, the hotel is old, and not all the rooms are in the latest style or display enviable taste, but it is clean and has enough charm to draw many repeats. The desk staff can be brusque if overworked, but if you can brush up on a few French words and phrases, they will usually end up by bending a little.

English Spoken: Most of the time

Facilities and Services: Direct-dial phones, elevator, TVs

Nearest Tourist Attraction (Right Bank): Passy

Hôtel Regina de Passy ★★★
6, rue de la Tour (16th)

TELEPHONE
45-24-43-64

TELEX
645-004 F

FAX
(1) 40-50-70-62

MÉTRO
Passy

CREDIT CARDS
AE, DC, MC, V

64 rooms, all with bath or shower and toilet

Built in 1930 for the International Exhibition, this wonderful hotel is high on the Right Bank of the Seine across from the Eiffel Tower. The Art Deco lobby has a graceful winding staircase framed by marvelous signed stained-glass windows. The newly restyled rooms are sophisticated and ultra-modern, while the older ones, still in excellent condition, retain the elegance of a gracious past. Eight of the rooms have small balconies overlooking the Passy neighborhood and the Eiffel Tower in the distance. The penthouse apartments with private rooftop terraces boast impressive furnishings, marble bathrooms (one with a sunken tub), small bars, fully equipped kitchens, and enough wardrobe space for most of us to unpack and stay a year. These apartments would be perfect for a small family or anyone on an extended stay. The management continually upgrades the hotel, and the staff is anxious to please in every way. A stay in this hotel would enhance any visit to Paris.

English Spoken: Yes

Facilities and Services: Air-conditioning in apartments, direct-dial phones, elevator, hair dryers, minibars, room safes, radios, TVs with international reception

Nearest Tourist Attractions (Right Bank): Passy, Trocadéro

RATES
1 or 2 persons 560–770F, apartment 875–1,212F; extra bed 160F (*Note:* Lower rates in July, August, January, December)

BREAKFAST
Continental, 40F

Hôtel Victor Hugo ★★★
19, rue Copernic (16th)

76 rooms, all with bath or shower and toilet

Returning guests appreciate the refined luxury offered by the modern Hôtel Victor Hugo. Owned since 1973 by M. and Mme Mullie, it is conveniently located next to the Place Victor-Hugo, home of the BCBGs (*bon chic, bon genre*—French yuppies) of Paris, and a good place to begin a shopping trip down the fashionable Avenue Victor-Hugo.

The tastefully detailed rooms have comfortable beds and chairs, generous table space, and modern marble baths. The fourth-floor rooms overlook the pretty bird-filled and tree-lined Copernic reservoir. The downstairs lobby is resplendent with leather furniture, fabric-covered walls, and leafy green plants. Beyond it is a comfortable bar and one of the prettiest breakfast rooms in Paris, situated in a stone grotto garden with a bubbling fountain and a canopied breakfast cart filled with tempting morning treats.

English Spoken: Yes

Facilities and Services: Bar, conference room, direct-dial phones, elevator, mini-bars, porter, radios, TVs with international reception

TELEPHONE
45-53-76-01, for reservations 45-53-14-91

TELEX
630-939 F

FAX
(1) 45-53-69-93

MÉTRO
Victor Hugo, Boissière

CREDIT CARDS
MC, V

RATES
Single 595–640F, double 665–720F, suite 1,105F, air-conditioned conference room 840F

BREAKFAST
Continental in room, 45F; downstairs buffet, 55F

Nearest Tourist Attractions (Right Bank): Shopping on Avenue Victor-Hugo, Trocadéro, Guimet Museum, Arc de Triomphe, Champs-Élysées

Le Hameau de Passy ★★
48, rue de Passy (16th)

TELEPHONE
42-88-47-55

TELEX
651-469 F

FAX
(1) 42-30-83-72

MÉTRO
Passy, La Muette

CREDIT CARDS
AE, MC, V

RATES
Single 475F, double 515–535F, triple 620F

BREAKFAST
Continental, included; hotel will deduct 20F per person if informed at beginning of stay that you won't take breakfast

32 rooms, all with bath or shower and toilet

Hidden in a garden walkway off the popular Rue de Passy, the new Hameau de Passy is a snappy two-star addition to this posh part of Paris. The owners of Hôtel de Passy Eiffel (see page 127) took this rumpled and worn-out hotel and completely transformed it into the modern four-building structure it is today. The rooms are all in the same style, with stark white walls, open closets, soft sheer curtains at the windows, and coordinated fabrics and carpets. If you are lucky and land in building No. 4, the elevator takes the strain out of climbing up three or four flights to your room. Otherwise, in buildings No. 1, 2, and 3, you will have to hike up a winding outdoor metal stairway that offers no protection from the elements. If this sort of exercise doesn't bother you and you want to be only a whisper away from all the great shopping in Passy, consider this hotel.

English Spoken: Yes

Facilities and Services: Direct-dial phones, elevator *only* to building No. 4, TVs with international reception

Nearest Tourist Attractions (Right Bank): Passy, Trocadéro

Résidence Chambellan Morgane ★★★
6, rue Keppler (16th)

TELEPHONE
47-20-35-72

TELEX
613-682 F

FAX
(1) 47-20-95-69

MÉTRO
Kléber

CREDIT CARDS
AE, DC, MC, V

20 rooms, all with bath or shower and toilet

In 1984, when I began writing *Cheap Sleeps in Paris*, I fell in love with a little hotel in the 16th arrondissement called the Résidence Morgane. It was run by a grandmotherly woman who paid close attention to her guests and pampered them beyond the call of duty. She would make an omelette at midnight, keep your messages, forward mail, and do your laundry and ironing if asked. When I returned a year or so later, it was obvious that Madame was gone and the hotel was being run by a non-caring staff. On a hunch, I decided to recheck the hotel. I am glad I did. Although Madame is not back, the new owners and their professional staff work hard to please their international clientele. In addition, the new owners have masterminded a much-needed renovation project that has turned the old hotel into the epitome of three-star elegance and classic luxury.

The lobby and entrance mix American Southwestern colors with white enamel woodwork and beautifully upholstered Louis XV-style antiques. Light pumpkin-colored halls lead to stylishly outfitted bedrooms with silk wall coverings, matching quilted spreads and curtains, and efficient mirrored and marbled bathrooms. Now, as once before, I warmly recommend this hotel for a quiet and romantic stay close to the Champs-Élysées.

English Spoken: Yes

Facilities and Services: Bar, direct-dial phones, elevator, hair dryers, mini-bars, TVs, radios, clocks, room service for light meals

Nearest Tourist Attractions (Right Bank): Champs-Élysées, Arc de Triomphe, shopping on Avenue Victor-Hugo

RATES
1 or 2 persons 585–875F

BREAKFAST
Continental (with juice and cheese), 45F; the works (with bacon and eggs), 65F

SEVENTEENTH ARRONDISSEMENT

Wide leafy boulevards characterize this subdued and upscale residential *quartier*. The main attraction for anyone staying in this area is the quiet and the close proximity to the Palais des Congrès, a convention center with restaurants, movie theaters, and the pick-up and drop-off point for passengers to and from Charles de Gaulle airport.

SEVENTEENTH ARRONDISSEMENT
Right Bank: Palais des Congrès

HOTELS IN THE SEVENTEENTH ARRONDISSEMENT
Hôtel Astrid ★★★
Hôtel Belidor ★
Hôtel de Banville ★★★

Hôtel de Neuville ★★★
Hôtel des Deux Acacias ★★
Hôtel Eber ★★★
Hôtel Étoile Péreire ★★★
Hôtel Flaubert ★★
Hôtel Palma ★★
Hôtel Regent's Garden ★★★
Résidence Levis Hôtel ★★

Hôtel Astrid ★★★
27, avenue Carnot (17th)

41 rooms, all with bath or shower and toilet

TELEPHONE
43-80-56-20
TELEX
642-065 F
FAX
(1) 47-63-37-02
MÉTRO
Charles-de-Gaulle Étoile
CREDIT CARDS
AE, MC, V
RATES
Single 385–460F, double 410–550F
BREAKFAST
Continental, included; cannot be deducted

At the family-run Hôtel Astrid, you will pay a moderate price for living in this top-drawer *quartier* of Paris. The colors used throughout are cheerfully appropriate and blend well with the modern furnishings. Two of the nicest bedrooms have small balconies for viewing the Arc de Triomphe. The rooms are upgraded on a continual basis, and I recommend that you ask for one of the newest when reserving. Breakfast is included in the price of the room, making the price even more of a bargain. An additional advantage of the hotel is that it is only about a five-minute walk to the Air France bus stop for Charles de Gaulle airport, so if you don't have much luggage or you have a luggage trolley, you can save additional money on cab fare.

English Spoken: Yes

Facilities and Services: Direct-dial phones, elevator, hair dryers, TVs with international reception

Nearest Tourist Attractions (Right Bank): Étoile, Arc de Triomphe

Hôtel Belidor ★
5, rue Belidor (17th)

42 rooms, 17 with bath or shower and toilet

TELEPHONE
45-74-49-91
TELEX
None
FAX
(1) 45-72-54-22

No serious Cheap Sleeper should overlook the Belidor. Despite a plastic floral arrangement here and there and an eccentric assortment of trinkets in the reception and breakfast rooms, there is no shortage of the kind of charm that comes with years of graceful aging. The Belidor will provide you with a clean bed in a decent residential neighborhood just around the corner from the Palais des Congrès. The rooms are all as neat as pins, and those with baths are larger than many three-star rooms at twice or three times the price. Don't let the out-of-the-way location deter you, because after only a ten-minute Métro ride you can be standing in the Louvre, floating down the Seine on a *bateau mouche*, or strolling through the most romantic streets of St-Germain-des-Prés. It is crucial that you plan ahead for this one—the rooms are booked weeks in advance all during the year.

English Spoken: Some

Facilities and Services: Direct-dial phones, no elevator

Nearest Tourist Attractions (Right Bank): Palais des Congrès exhibition center; all other tourist attractions require public transportation

MÉTRO
Porte Maillot, *sorti côté pairs* (exit on even-numbered side of street)

CREDIT CARDS
None; cash only, paid in advance

RATES
Single 130–235F, double 155–355F; hall shower 20F

BREAKFAST
Continental, 30F; included, but can be deducted if requested in advance

Hôtel de Banville ★★★
166, boulevard Berthier (17th)
39 rooms, all with bath or shower and toilet

The classic Hôtel de Banville is my idea of a wonderful Parisian hotel. It was built in 1928 by architect Jerome Bellat, who designed many of the magnificent Art Deco buildings the 17th arrondissement is famous for. Despite its location on the fringes of things, good public transportation is close, and so are several well-priced restaurants (see *Cheap Eats in Paris*).

Recent redecorating projects include a new lobby and dining area with hand-painted murals. Most of the rooms have been repainted, using an artistic technique that combines sponges and brushes. The result is beautiful and very soothing. The hotel has a large following of guests who enjoy the handsomely coordinated rooms. They also appreciate the efforts of owner Mme Lambert and her right-hand man, Jean-Pierre, to deal with the demands of their guests. Mme Lambert grew up in the hotel business, and all her family is involved in the industry in some way. Her background and expertise, combined with her impeccably

TELEPHONE
42-67-70-16

TELEX
H BANVIL 643-025 F

FAX
(1) 44-40-42-77

MÉTRO
Péreire, Porte-de-Champerret

CREDIT CARDS
AE, MC, V

RATES
Single 550F, double 600F, triple 715F, quad 740F

BREAKFAST
Continental, 35F; *dietetique* (whole-wheat bread; hard- or soft-boiled egg or yogurt or cornflakes; juice; coffee or tea) 60F; *pleine forme* (pastries; yogurt, cheese, or cereal; 2 eggs, ham, sausage or meat pie; fruit juice and coffee; tea or chocolate) 75F

good taste, show throughout the hotel. From the welcoming lobby to the imaginative rooms filled with family antiques and heirlooms, you can tell immediately that this is a hotel where the owner knows what she is doing. All of the rooms are lovely, but for an extra-special experience, ask for No. 82 or No. 83, each with a sweeping postcard view from the Arc de Triomphe to La Tour Montparnasse.

English Spoken: Yes, and German

Facilities and Services: Direct-dial phones, elevator to all but top floor, hair dryers, room service for light snacks, radios, TVs with international reception

Nearest Tourist Attractions (Right Bank): None; must use public transportation

Hôtel de Neuville ★★★
3, place Verniquet and boulevard Péreire (17th)
28 rooms, all with bath or shower and toilet

TELEPHONE
43-80-26-30, 43-80-38-55

TELEX
648-822 F

FAX
(1) 43-80-38-55

MÉTRO
Péreire

CREDIT CARDS
AE, DC, MC, V

RATES
Single 570F, double 665F; extra bed 160F (special low-season, business, weekend, and group rates)

BREAKFAST
Continental, 40F

Monsieur Bigeard, the former owner of the popular Quai d'Orsay restaurant, transformed this frayed 19th-century building into a smart hotel. Since its opening, the Neuville has been doing exceptionally well because of his enlightened approach to modern hotel management. There should be more hotels like this: where service counts, and attention to detail is taken very seriously.

The stunning lobby overlooks an imaginative two-level garden. A small restaurant, showcasing M. Bigeard's cooking skills, looks out onto the garden's lower level. This welcoming room is done in greens and yellows, with trellised wallpaper, matching table covers, and a live green plant on each table. The beautifully appointed rooms blend coordinated fabrics with white-washed furniture, mirrored wardrobes, and good bathrooms. Across the street from the hotel is a leafy neighborhood square with benches for sitting and tennis courts that guests can use for 100F per hour. The only drawback I can see to this unusually nice hotel is its location far from tourist central, but for some this may only add to its charm.

English Spoken: Yes, also German and Polish

Facilities and Services: Bar, direct-dial phones,

elevator, restaurant serving lunch and dinner Mon–Fri and breakfast daily, radios, TVs, tennis courts across from hotel, 100F per hour

Nearest Tourist Attractions (Right Bank): None; must use public transportation; about a 10-minute walk from the hotel

Hôtel des Deux Acacias ★★
28, rue de l'Arc-de-Triomphe (17th)
31 rooms, all with bath or shower and toilet

Despite the rather plain atmosphere, this Cheap Sleep cannot be ignored by visitors wanting to keep within a certain budget and still be conveniently close to the Champs-Élysées. The hotel is owned by Mme Delmas, who took over from her parents when they retired almost 60 years ago. Her gentle demeanor permeates the entire operation, with the exception of the sometimes austere welcome from the matronly manager and her dour husband.

No one could ever call this modest place modern, but the spotless large rooms are color coordinated, well ventilated, and have generous closet and luggage space. Two small student rooms on the top floor are in great demand for long stays and must be reserved months in advance. Enclosed public parking is available across the street for motorists.

English Spoken: No

Facilities and Services: Direct-dial phones, elevator, TVs

Nearest Tourist Attractions (Right Bank): Champs-Élysées. Arc de Triomphe

TELEPHONE
43-80-01-85

TELEX
None

FAX
(1) 40-53-94-62

MÉTRO
Charles-de-Gaulle Étoile

CREDIT CARDS
V

RATES
Single 310F, double 310–355F, triple 540F

BREAKFAST
Continental, 25F

Hôtel Eber ★★★
18, rue Léon-Jost (17th)
18 rooms, all with bath or shower and toilet

Travelers longing for peace and quiet have at their disposal a group of French hotels whose owners have taken a vow of silence. The Hôtel Eber is one of the 275 members of Relais du Silence, an association of individually owned hotels dedicated to providing a silent and peaceful atmosphere where guests can feel at home.

TELEPHONE
46-22-60-70

TELEX
649-949 F NONCOUR

FAX
(1) 47-63-01-01

MÉTRO
Courcelles

CREDIT CARDS
AE, DC. MC, V

RATES
1 or 2 persons 580–630F,
apartment for 1 or 2 persons
1,000–1,260F
BREAKFAST
Continental, 45F

At the Eber, the entrance along a tiled walkway opens onto a small beamed salon centered around a carved fireplace. To the left of the reception desk is an inviting bar and breakfast area with comfortable armchairs. In the back is a leafy green patio with metal tables and chairs set in the summer for al fresco breakfasts. The rooms are decorated in light beiges and have good-looking art prints and posters on the walls. In its other life, years ago, the hotel was a bordello, so you can see that things have improved drastically.

English Spoken: Yes

Facilities and Services: Bar, direct-dial phones, elevator, hair dryers, mini-bars, TVs with international reception

Nearest Tourist Attractions (Right Bank): Can walk to Étoile and Champs-Élysées, but must use public transportation for all else

Hôtel Étoile Péreire ★★★
146, boulevard Péreire (17th)
26 rooms, all with bath or shower and toilet

TELEPHONE
42-67-60-00
TELEX
305-551 BSC ÉTOILE
FAX
(1) 42-67-02-90
MÉTRO
Péreire
CREDIT CARDS
AE, DC, MC, V
RATES
Single 485–600F, double 685F,
duplex 945F; extra bed for 1,
160F, extra bed for 2, 315F
BREAKFAST
Continental (cheese, juice, and
selection of 35 jams), 55F

The Étoile Péreire is a sophisticated hotel offering modern luxury at affordable prices. Occupying a distinctive building that is hard to identify as a hotel, it benefitted from a long-overdue remodeling project in 1987. Gone are the 1900s-style rooms and the bathtubs with feet, but not the peace and quiet the location affords or the dedicated services of the staff headed for so many years by Ferruccio Pardi.

The crisp rooms offer guests a mixture of modern Italian furniture and country fabrics in the Laura Ashley vein. The best bets are the two-story duplexes with ceiling fans, skylights, and soft watercolor paintings. M. Pardi prides himself on his breakfasts, which offer a vast selection of pure jams and jellies as well as fresh orange or grapefruit juices to accompany the croissants. You can even order ham or bacon and eggs if you are really starved.

While not in the tourist mainstream, the hotel is close to the Porte Maillot convention center and the Air France terminal. A pretty park with tennis courts is across the street and several old favorites listed in *Cheap Eats in Paris* are in the *quartier*.

English Spoken: Yes, and Italian

Facilities and Services: Direct-dial phones, mini-bars in most rooms, TVs with international reception

Nearest Tourist Attractions (Right Bank): None, must use public transportation

Hôtel Flaubert ★★
19, rue Rennequin (17th)
36 rooms, all with bath or shower and toilet

This upbeat garden hotel, designed and built by Christiane and Michel Niceron, opened its doors to its first guests in January 1989. Warm toast tones and airy bamboo furniture set the stage in the inviting lobby and breakfast rooms, which face onto a garden filled with blooming hydrangeas, impatiens, and colorful pansies. Singles or couples without much luggage should reserve one of the rooms opening onto this garden. For more space and better lighting, I like a top-floor *chambre*. The Nicerons are gracious hosts and work very hard to please their guests. They keep the rooms perfectly clean, the bathroom towels are thick, and their staff is pleasant. Judging from their record, repeat visitors will continue to fill their hotel for years to come.

English Spoken: Yes

Facilities and Services: Direct-dial phones, elevator, mini-bars, TVs

Nearest Tourist Attractions (Right Bank): Arc de Triomphe, Champs-Élysées

TELEPHONE
46-22-44-35

TELEX
649-689 F

FAX
(1) 43-80-32-34

MÉTRO
Ternes

CREDIT CARDS
MC, V

RATES
Single 330–440F, double 390–650F, triple 750F

BREAKFAST
Continental, 35F

Hôtel Palma ★★
46, rue Brunel (17th)
37 rooms, all with bath or shower and toilet

If you want the most for your battered Yankee buck and don't mind being a bit far from the center of things, the Palma is by far one of the best Cheap Sleeps deals in the French capital. Its fantastic value, coupled with its quality and quantity of service, delights the Palma's many followers. Located in the leafy precincts of the upper-crust 17th arrondissement, it is

TELEPHONE
45-74-74-51

TELEX
644-183 F

FAX
(1) 45-74-40-90

MÉTRO
Argentine

CREDIT CARDS
MC, V

RATES
Single 355–375F, double 375F, triple 455F
BREAKFAST
Continental, 35F

within an easy walk to the Palais des Congrés exhibition center, the Air France terminal at Porte Maillot, and excellent public transportation links that will whisk you anyplace you want to be in less than 30 minutes.

The best thing about this undiscovered treasure, besides its value and the congenial owners M. and Mme Couderc, is that guests never have the feeling they are "budgeting" by staying here. Nothing is torn or tattered, no carpets are frayed, everything that should be painted is, the furnishings are exceptionally nice, and every room has a nice bathroom and color TV with international reception. The rooms in highest demand are the blissfully quiet and cozy top-floor roosts with skylight views and slanting ceilings, and the two ground-floor rooms off the lobby.

English Spoken: Yes

Facilities and Services: Direct-dial phones, elevator, TVs with international reception

Nearest Tourist Attractions (Right Bank): Arc de Triomphe, Champs-Élysées, Palais des Congrès

Hôtel Regent's Garden ★★★
6, rue Pierre-Demours (17th)

TELEPHONE
45-74-07-30; toll free in U.S. and Canada: 800-528-1234
TELEX
640-127 F GARDEN
FAX
(1) 40-55-01-42
MÉTRO
Ternes, Charles-de-Gaulle Étoile, exit Rue Carnot
CREDIT CARDS
AE, DC, MC, V
RATES
Single 630–810F, double 670–930F, triple 950F
BREAKFAST
Continental, 40F

40 rooms, all with bath or shower and toilet

Originally built by Napoléon III for his personal physician, this building is now a refined garden hotel. Hidden behind a high brick wall, it seems a little far from the hub of things, but, in fact, Rue Pierre-Demours is only a few minutes' walk from the Champs-Élysées and the Arc de Triomphe.

The cavernous, high-ceilinged rooms have crystal chandeliers, decorative moldings, marble fireplaces, brass bedsteads, floor-to-ceiling mirrors, and authentic period furnishings. Many rooms connect for family stays, and several have large walk-in closets with built-in shelves and shoe racks. The bathrooms are all thoroughly 20th century and luxuriously fitted with fluffy terry cloth robes, scented bubble bath, and hair dryers. Most rooms overlook the garden, which is landscaped with large trees, stone statues, flowering walkways, and a terrace with tables for summer breakfasts or afternoon teas.

Everyone who has ever stayed at the Regent's Garden loves it and you will too, because it offers affordable elegance, with an ambience of bygone days in Paris. The prices are high, but worth it for the beautiful stay.

English Spoken: Yes

Facilites and Services: Direct-dial phones, elevator, hair dryers, mini-bars, parking 45F (first-come basis), radios, TVs with international reception

Nearest Tourist Attractions (Right Bank): Champs-Élysées, Arc de Triomphe, Palais des Congrès exhibition center

Résidence Levis Hôtel ★★
16, rue Lebouteux (17th)

10 rooms, 3 with bath or shower and toilet, 7 with shower and no toilet

If location isn't your first concern, but money is, the ten-room Résidence Levis is worth serious thought. In an area restfully free of tourists and definitely more than a heartbeat away from much action, by Métro it is only a few stops from all the bright lights and low life in Montmartre and Pigalle. Closer to home, shophounds and camera buffs will enjoy the animated shops and hawkers along Rue de Levis. It isn't the place for finding *haute* anything, but it is a slice of Parisian middle-class life worth experiencing. As for the hotel's rooms, they are large and the colors blend, although the decor includes large-patterned, vivid-colored wallpaper, fifties-style furniture, and more than a fair dose of chenille. Never mind—the place is as clean as any you will find, and the owner is sweet and helpful. Let's face it: the bottom line is what counts, and the price here is kind to most budgets, allowing guests to spend their sleeping money doing more interesting things in Paris.

English Spoken: Yes

Facilities and Services: Bar, direct-dial phones, elevator

Nearest Tourist Attractions (Right Bank): None; must use public transportation

TELEPHONE
47-63-86-38

TELEX
None

FAX
None

MÉTRO
Villiers

CREDIT CARDS
MC, V

RATES
1 or 2 persons, 330–380F

BREAKFAST
Continental, 30F

EIGHTEENTH ARRONDISSEMENT

Montmartre is a rambling *quartier* full of contrasts, combining picture-postcard quaintness and razzle-dazzle. It was here that Toulouse-Lautrec drew the cancan girls dancing at the Moulin Rouge, and where Picasso and Braque created cubism at the Bateau-Lavoir. The panoramic view from the steps of Sacré-Coeur at dawn or sunset, the many artists' ateliers, and the intimate village atmosphere that prevails along the narrow streets, many of which are the same as when Utrillo painted them, continue to evoke the dynamic spirit and colorful past of this vibrant part of Paris. It is a must stop for any visitor wanting to absorb the spirit of Paris, both present and past.

HOTELS IN THE EIGHTEENTH ARRONDISSEMENT
Ermitage Hôtel ★★
Hôtel le Bouquet Montmartre ★★
Hôtel Prima Lepic ★★
Timhôtel Montmartre ★★

Ermitage Hôtel ★★
24, rue Lamarck (18th)

TELEPHONE
42-64-79-22

TELEX
None

FAX
(1) 42-64-10-33

MÉTRO
Lamarck-Caulaincourt

CREDIT CARDS
None; cash only

RATES
Single 330F, double 380F, triple 470F, quad 550F

BREAKFAST
Continental, included; served in bed if requested

17 rooms, all with bath or shower and toilet

Close your eyes and imagine being in Paris and waking up in an antiques-filled hotel high atop Montmartre with magical views over the entire city. Sound wonderful? It does, and it is all possible at the Ermitage, a poetic refuge run by the engaging Maggie Canipel and her husband. In the late 1970s, the couple sold everything they had and bought the Ermitage. They updated the plumbing, filled the old mansion with their collection of fine furniture, and began welcoming guests, continually outdoing themselves to make everyone feel at home.

Any one of their rooms could steal your heart, but my favorites are No. 6 and No. 10, on the top floor, with tall French windows opening onto the morning sun and views of all Paris; and No. 11 and No. 12, which open onto a beautiful terrace garden.

True, you will need strong legs and lungs to walk up the hill from the Métro, but once there, you will be in the center of one of the most picturesque parts of Paris. You can wander the streets once painted by Utrillo, peek into artists' ateliers, and have your portrait painted by one of the pseudo-artists lining the touristy Place du Tertre. Undiscovered restaurants in all price ranges are within walking distance (see *Cheap Eats in Paris*).

English Spoken: Yes, also German and Italian

Facilities and Services: Direct-dial phones, no elevator

Nearest Tourist Attractions (Right Bank): Montmartre

Hôtel le Bouquet de Montmartre ★★
1, rue Durantin (18th)

36 rooms, all with shower, 22 with bath or shower and toilet

If you are an exacting guest, this hotel is probably not for you. If, on the other hand, you are a committed Cheap Sleeper with a fondness for Montmartre, read on. For visitors who want to experience the fun and the village atmosphere of the area and still stay under budget, the Bouquet de Montmartre is a little honey of a hotel. Its second-floor lobby may be difficult to find, but the search is worth it.

The Gibergues family works hard to keep this Victorian hotel as nice as it is for the price. Most of the small rooms fall into the "cute" category, with lacy curtains and brightly tiled baths in purple, lavender, royal blue, and aqua. An ornate dining room with red velvet chairs, lacquered furniture, and globe lights reminds you that you are indeed in Montmartre.

From the hotel you can stroll in any direction and see something interesting. You can climb up to Sacré-Coeur, or crawl down the hill and view the underside of Paris on full display in Pigalle. For longer trips, jump on the Montmartobus, a minibus service that plies the winding streets snaking around the Butte. You can ride from the bottom at Pigalle to the end of

TELEPHONE
46-06-87-54

TELEX
None

FAX
None

MÉTRO
Abbesses

CREDIT CARDS
None; cash only

RATES
Single 290–330F, double 210–330F, triple 390–420F, quad 460F

BREAKFAST
Continental, 30F

the line at Métro Jules Joffrin. Stop along the route if something intrigues you and get back on—it will be one of the most pleasurable rides you will take in Paris.

English Spoken: No

Facilities and Services: Direct-dial phones, no elevator, hotel closes and locks front door from 2:30 A.M.–7:30 A.M. and guests do not have keys during this time

Nearest Tourist Attractions (Right Bank): Montmartre

Hôtel Prima-Lepic ★★
29, rue Lepic (18th)

46-06-44-64

TELEX
281-162 F

FAX
(1) 46-06-66-11

MÉTRO
Abbesses

CREDIT CARDS
MC, V

RATES
Single 275F, double 360F, triple 400F, apartment 485–845F

BREAKFAST
Buffet, 35F

38 rooms, all with bath or shower and toilet

The Prima-Lepic is a century-old Montmartre building that still has its ornate ceiling moldings, marble fireplaces, and a corner cherub or two for good measure. Appealing to a young, international clientele on slim budgets, the hotel is a good base for exploring Montmartre.

It looks very nice from the outside, painted white with balconies overlooking the busy market street that runs the length of Rue Lepic. The welcoming entry overlooks a tromp l'oeil English garden that sets the floral theme for the main floor of the hotel. The beamed breakfast area has a fabulous mural depicting life in Montmartre, and floral prints by Monet.

Many of the rooms have recently benefitted from long-overdue redecorating. When reserving, request any room that faces front on the third, fourth, or fifth floor, because they have balconies and more light. They also have noise. In a room on the back, you will get more space, but less light and no view at all. These are, of course, the quieter choices. The apartments are spacious enough, but not recommended because they are dark and gloomy and have grim views on the back side of the building.

English Spoken: Yes

Facilities and Services: Direct-dial phones, elevator, hair dryers, TVs

Nearest Tourist Attractions (Right Bank):
Montmartre

Timhôtel Montmartre ★★
11, rue Ravignan (Place Émile Goudeau) (18th)
63 rooms, all with bath or shower and toilet

See page 35 for general information on all the Timhôtels.

This Timhôtel is one of the best in the chain, if only for its picturesque location on the pretty Place Émile Goudeau. If you ask for a fourth or fifth floor room with a view, you will be able to see all of Paris, including the Eiffel Tower.

Other nice rooms face the Place Émile Goudeau and have views of the tip of Sacré Coeur. Note: The singles are very, very tiny.

English Spoken: Yes

Facilities and Services: Bar, direct-dial phones, elevator, baby cots and changing tables, irons and ironing boards, radios, TVs with international reception, videos

Nearest Tourist Attractions (Right Bank): Montmartre

TELEPHONE
42-55-74-79

TELEX
650-508 F

FAX
(1) 42-55-71-01

MÉTRO
Abbesses

RATES
Single 325F, double 405–445F; extra bed 110F

BREAKFAST
Continental; in room 45F, downstairs 35F

OTHER OPTIONS

If the hotel life isn't for you, there are other options available in Paris. Consider a return to nature—i.e., camping—or perhaps staying as a paying guest in a private home and experiencing the Parisians on their own turf. Another cost-saving possibility is renting your own studio or apartment. The benefits are numerous, from having more space to spread out, to shopping for your own food and getting to know the local merchants better. Finally, there are the myriad of options available to students from 15- to 75-years-old.

CAMPING OUT
Les Campings du Bois de Bologne

RENTING A PRIVATE APARTMENT
Chez Vous
Rothray

RESIDENCE HOTELS
Citadines Trocadéro
Home Plazza Résidence Hôtels: Bastille and Nation
Pierre et Vacances: Résidence Charles Dullin

STAYING IN A PRIVATE HOME
Bed & Breakfast 1
International Café-Couette

STUDENT ACCOMMODATIONS

CAMPING OUT

Les Campings du Bois de Boulogne
Allée du Bord de l'Eau (16th)

While Coleman stoves, tents, inflatable mattresses, and citronella candles are not on everyone's packing list for Paris, they might be on yours if you plan to camp out there. Yes, it *is* possible! Les Campings in the Bois de Boulogne is on the far edge of the park and provides the only truly rustic opportunity for Cheap Sleeps in Paris. Geared mostly to students and hearty international travelers, or those with RVs, the campground is located 4 kilometers away from the nearest Métro, making it almost essential that you have your own set of wheels, or don't mind walking if the camp bus schedule doesn't correspond with your plans to go into Paris. Accommodations vary, from tent sites to RV hookups. A convenience store, a money changer, hot showers, a washer and dryer, and, from April through October, bus service to Paris and a restaurant are open to aid campers. The office is open from 6 A.M. until 2 A.M., and accepts *no* reservations for campsites, but does accept them if you want to make a mobile home booking. Everything is always on a first-come-first-served basis.

English Spoken: Limited

Facilities and Services: Convenience store, money changer, information office, washing machines, hot showers, bus service to Paris and restaurant open April–October

Nearest Tourist Attractions: None

TELEPHONE
45-24-30-00

TELEX
None

FAX
None

MÉTRO
Porte-Maillot (4 km from campground) (Take bus No. 244 from Porte-Maillot, get off at Route des Moulins, and walk down path on right. Do not follow misleading signs to left on main road.)

CREDIT CARDS
None; cash only

RATES
Campsite: 1 tent, 2 persons 60F per night, RV hookups for 2 persons 75F, RV hookup with water and TV for 4 persons 155F, extra person in tent or RV 20F; mobile home: first 3 nights, 450F per night, after 3 nights 385F per night

RENTING A PRIVATE APARTMENT

Chez Vous
220 Redwood Highway, Ste. 129
Mill Valley, CA 94941 USA

A stay in a Chez Vous accommodation will allow you to actually *live* in Paris, not just visit. These impressive private homes and apartments are located

TELEPHONE
(415) 331-2535

TELEX
None

FAX
(415) 331-5296 (in the U.S.)
(*Note*: All reservations and
inquiries for Chez Vous should
be made through U.S. office)
CREDIT CARDS
AE, MC, V
RATES
Varies with accommodation
BREAKFAST
Available in a B&B only

in only the best sections of Paris, not in marginal, out-of-the-way, or uninteresting *quartiers* of the city. The possibilities range from self-contained houses in the posh 16th to studios around Place des Vosges. Each place is lightly stocked with food, fresh flowers are on the dining room table, and every guest is met at their rental by an English-speaking member of the Chez Vous staff. If you are venturing outside of Paris, and this type of stay appeals to you, ask about their catalog of rental properties throughout France, called *At Home in France*. They also offer bed and breakfast accommodations in private farmhouses, manor homes, and chateaux throughout France, but not in Paris. The catalog for this is *Bed & Breakfast: French Style*.

English Spoken: Yes

Facilities and Services: Varies with accommodation

Nearest Tourist Attractions: Depends on location of accommodation

Rothray
10, rue Nicolas-Flamel (4th)

TELEPHONE
48-87-13-37
TELEX
614-806 F
FAX
(1) 40-26-34-33
MÉTRO
Châtelet
CREDIT CARDS
None; cash or personal U.S.
checks
RATES
Rates from 550–1,100F per
day, less by month. Prices vary
according to size and location
of apartment, as well as length
of stay; minimum 7-day stay
required
BREAKFAST
Not available

Some short-term private apartment rentals in Paris can be potluck affairs that offer unwelcome surprises on arrival: strange shabby decor, varying amenities and levels of cleanliness, and haphazard services by the agency in charge. You will find none of these in an apartment rented through Rothray. Competently owned and managed by Ray Lambard and his partner Roth, Rothray, in my opinion, offers the best apartment rentals in Paris for the short-term visitor or for someone on a long assignment.

Most of their apartments are located in peaceful sections of neighborhoods where a stroll around a corner will put historic Paris at your fingertips. After a few days you will discover what living in Paris is all about, and probably spend part of your time trying to make more permanent arrangements, or figuring out how to return more often. It will be love at first sight when you walk into one of Rothray's tastefully furnished and beautifully equipped apartments. In addition to the attractive furnishings, all have cable TV, stereo systems, and American-style kitchens, which you can only fully appreciate if you have ever tried to prepare a meal in a French closet-style kitchen. Some even have washers, dryers, and dishwashers. Weekly maid service, linen changes, and a refrigerator stocked with fruit juices, wine, and beer are included.

English Spoken: Yes

Facilities and Services: Services are the best; facilities vary from one apartment to another, but are all excellent

Nearest Tourist Attractions: Varies by apartment

RESIDENCE HOTELS

Citadines Trocadéro
29 bis, rue St-Didier (16th)

66 accommodations ranging from small studettes to full-sized apartments

Citadines offers three locations. The best is Trocadéro, because it is close to everything on a tourist's agenda. There are several possibilities, ranging from a miniscule studette to a nice-sized apartment. Frankly, the studettes and studios are just too small for any degree of long-term comfort, but the apartments have adequate living space. All types of facilities are furnished with an equipped kitchenette, a full bath with plenty of shelf space, a color TV, weekly linen changes, and a direct-dial telephone. You must do your own housekeeping, unless you opt for maid service, which is extra. Baby beds, an iron and ironing board, and a vacuum cleaner are provided free of charge. There is a coin-operated washing machine and dryer in the basement. Stays can range from a few days to several months, but the longer the stay, the lower the price, especially during the off season. Just a block away is one of the best supermarket complexes in Paris, where every household shopping need can be met.

English Spoken: Yes

Facilities and Services: Direct-dial phones, elevator, gym, baby beds, irons and ironing boards, vacu-

TELEPHONE
47-04-88-02

TELEX
CITROCA 640-464 F

FAX
(1) 47-04-50-07

MÉTRO
Victor Hugo

CREDIT CARDS
AE, DC, MC, V

RATES
Generally 450–1,450F; parking 50F per day, 1,000F per month (Rental prices vary according to size and type of accommodation, length of stay, and season)

BREAKFAST
Not available

ums, sauna, TVs, dishwashers in all but studettes, parking, weekly linen changes, maid service (100F per hour!), coin-operated washers and dryers

Nearest Tourist Attractions (Right Bank): Shopping on Avenue Victor-Hugo, Arc de Triomphe, Champs-Élysées

Home Plazza Résidence Hôtels: Bastille and Nation ★★★

CREDIT CARDS
AE, DC, MC, V
RATES
550–1,600F per day; parking
95F per day (Rental rates vary according to season, number of persons, and length of stay)
BREAKFAST
Continental, 55F

The two Home Plazza residences are located in a part of Paris which, until a few years ago, was considered a tourist wilderness. Now it is close to the thick of things in the Marais and Bastille near the new Opéra building. These residence hotels offer equipped studios and apartments furnished in a simple modern style that hold up well under hard use. One of the major benefits of staying here is all the extras available to the guest. These include a conference and business center featuring a multilingual secretarial staff, and offices to rent for a day or a month. At the Bastille location there is a nice patio restaurant and bar, a fitness center with a sauna, a Jacuzzi, and a gym, and, at both, a full complement of uniformed staff to cater to your every need and want. Twenty percent of the rooms in each are reserved exclusively for nonsmokers. In a country that lives in a constant Gauloise-cigarette-induced haze, this is a miracle!

Home Plazza Bastille ★★★
74, rue Amelot (11th)

TELEPHONE
40-21-20-00
TELEX
HOMEPLA 211-764 F
FAX
(1) 47-00-82-40
MÉTRO
St-Sebastien-Froissart

288 studios and apartments, fully furnished with equipped kitchens

See the general information immediately above.
English Spoken: Yes
Facilities and Services: Bar, conference room, direct-dial phones, elevator, hair dryers, parking 95F per day, room safes, restaurant for lunch and dinner Mon–Sat, radios, TVs with international reception

Nearest Tourist Attractions (Right Bank): Marais, Bastille

Home Plazza Nation ★★★
289 bis, rue du Faubourg St-Antoine (11th)

90 studios and apartments, fully furnished with equipped kitchens

See the general information above.

English Spoken: Yes

Facilities and Services: Conference room, direct-dial phones, elevator, hair dryers, parking 95F per day, safes in studios and apts, radios, TVs with international reception, weekly maid service

Nearest Tourist Attractions (Right Bank): None, must use Métro

TELEPHONE
40-09-40-00

TELEX
HOMPLA 240-303 F

FAX
(1) 40-09-11-55

MÉTRO
Nation

Pierre et Vacances: Résidence Charles Dullin, Montmartre ★★★
10, place Charles-Dullin (18th)

76 studios or apartments

I like to recommend the Résidence Charles Dullin as a home-away-from-home for those who want to explore Paris from a typical neighborhood. This part of Montmartre is full of contrasts. By day, it is interesting for its many colorful local characters who wander the streets and sit and reminisce in the cafés. In the evening, the atmosphere changes and it becomes young and alive until the wee hours with Parisians and tourists eating and drinking in the many bistros and restaurants, which offer every kind of cuisine from African couscous to Yugoslavian pork stews and health burgers.

From a practical standpoint, everything you will need to set up short- or long-term housekeeping is within an easy five- or ten-minute walk: small supermarkets, banks, a main post office, pharmacies, a dry cleaner, a shoe repair shop, a photo store, pungent cheese shops, tempting *boulangeries*, colorful fish and meat markets, and one of the best shopping streets in this part of Paris, Rue Lepic.

The 76 studios and apartments are, for the most part, spacious and livable. All have kitchens and a uniformity of services and facilities. Weekly maid service *is* included, as are linen and towel changes

TELEPHONE
42-57-14-55

TELEX
290-532 F

FAX
(1) 42-54-48-87

MÉTRO
Abbesses, Anvers

CREDIT CARDS
AE, DC, MC, V

RATES
Generally 590–1,170F per day; parking 65F per day, 365F per week; maid service 65F per hour (Rental rates vary according to size and type of accommodation, length of stay, and season)

BREAKFAST
Continental, 42F

twice weekly. If you want more frequent maid service, there is an hourly charge. The best part is, the longer the stay, the lower the price, especially in the low season.

English Spoken: Yes

Facilities and Services: Direct-dial phones, elevator, parking, TVs, maid service

Nearest Tourist Attractions (Right Bank): Montmartre

STAYING IN A PRIVATE HOME OR APARTMENT

Bed and Breakfast 1

TELEPHONE
43-25-43-97
TELEX
None
FAX
(1) 43-54-47-56
MÉTRO
Vavin
CREDIT CARDS
None; cash only
RATES
Bed & breakfast: Single 210–350F, double 130–225F; apartments: 1 or 2 persons 350–600F, 3 or 4 persons 400–800F
BREAKFAST
Included with bed and breakfast

73, rue Notre-Dame-des-Champs (6th)

Live in Paris like a Parisian with Bed and Breakfast 1. This organization prides itself on matching visitors and their bed and breakfast hosts according to tastes, age levels, and life styles. The star-rated rooms are true guest rooms in private homes, not just spare beds in back bedrooms. Prices vary, according to the type of accommodation and the location, which ranges from central Paris to the suburbs. Their apartments include all types, from the very simple to the luxurious, and are ideal alternatives for those wishing to spend less in restaurants and to shop for their food like Parisians. While it is always better to book ahead, you can also go to their Paris office and generally find something.

English Spoken: In office for bookings; depends on bed and breakfast

Facilities and Services: Varies with each accommodation

Nearest Tourist Attractions: Varies with each accommodation

International Café-Couette (Bed and Breakfast)

TELEPHONE
42-94-92-00
TELEX
281-311 CAFEC

8, rue d'Ilsy (8th) (must call ahead for appointment)

Personalize your visit and get to know the *real* Parisians by staying with them in their own homes.

This option is recommended for those who want to experience Paris on a more intimate and in-depth level. It is especially appealing to those who are fluent in French—or aspiring to be. The Café-Couette organization mails out a thick booklet detailing a full range of bed and breakfast possibilities in all sections of Paris, as well as throughout France. Each accommodation is graded, so you will know before you arrive if you will be in a modest sixth-floor walk-up in the Marais, or a lavish apartment in the 16th arrondissement. Prices vary accordingly.

English Spoken: Depends

Facilities and Services: Vary according to each accommodation

Nearest Tourist Attractions: Vary according to each accommodation

FAX
(1) 42-94-93-12

MÉTRO
St-Lazare (for office only)

CREDIT CARDS
None; plan to pay cash at each B&B

RATES
Vary according to each accommodation

BREAKFAST
Included

STUDENT ACCOMMODATIONS

There are more than 10,000 student beds available in Paris. The following list of possibilities is by no means complete, but offers a sampling of some of the best deals to get you started. It is critically important to remember that *only* cash is accepted at these student lodgings. For further information, contact any one of the addresses given below, or the French Government Tourist Office, 127, Champs-Élysées (8th), Métro Charles de Gaulle-Étoile, 47-23-61-72; open daily from 9 A.M.–6 P.M.

Any student can take advantage of the dozens of French government-run and/or subsidized student lodgings in Paris. In most cases you will be required to show proof of full-time student status; therefore, an International Student Identity Card is a smart investment. The card not only identifies you as a student, but entitles you to savings of up to 40 percent on museum entry fees, transportation, meals at certain student dining halls and much, much more. You can purchase the card in Paris at 119, rue St-Martin, (4th), Métro Rambuteau; open Monday through Friday from 9:30 A.M. to 6 P.M. If you purchase this ISIC card in the United States, you will derive further benefits including medical, accident, and hospital insurance. For more information on purchasing this true bargain in the United States, contact the Council on International Educational Exchange (CIEE), 205 East 42nd Street, 16th floor, New York, NY 10017; 212-421-3473.

If you are not a student but are under 26 years old, the Federation of International Youth Travel Organization (FIYTO) issues an International Youth Card. The card is internationally recognized and gives the holder access to literally thousands of discounts on everything from transportation, accommodations, and restaurants, to cultural activities and tours. In the United States the card is available from CIEE (see address and telephone number above).

Another option for saving lodging money is to become a member of the American Youth Hostels. For a list of their Parisian locations and any other information, write or call them at AYH, P.O. Box 37163, Washington, DC, 20013-7612, or call 202-783-6161.

FOYERS

Foyers (residential halls) do not belong to an international organization and may not require membership. UCRIF (Union des Centres de Rencontres Internationales de France) has nine lodging places in Paris. For the complete listing, contact the Maison de l'UCRIF, 4, rue Jean-Jacques Rousseau (1st), Métro Louvre, 42-60-42-40; open Monday through Friday 9 A.M. to 6 P.M. Arrive early for best selection.

Another *foyer* group is the Accueil des Jeunes in France (AJF), at 119, rue St-Martin (4th), Métro Rambuteau, 42-77-87-80; open Monday through Saturday 9:30 A.M. to 6 P.M. For best results in getting a good spot, arrive before 10 A.M., especially during the busy season. Some of their lodgings are located in historic central buildings; others are on the fringes, with long Métro commutes. Wherever you land, you will be required to pay in advance and not be able to see the room ahead of time. Breakfast is included, showers are free, and no written reservations are accepted. The age limit of 18 to 30 is sometimes overlooked in the off season. No curfew is enforced, and there is one to eight beds per room. If you are traveling elsewhere in France, ask for their thick book detailing a multitude of student possibilities throughout the country.

There are other *foyers* independent of group affiliation. All have their own characteristics, rules, and prices. For best results, call ahead or arrive when they open.

Association des Étudiants Protestants de Paris
46, rue de Vaugirard (6th)
Telephone: 43-54-31-49, 46-33-23-30
Métro: Luxembourg, Odéon

Open year round; 18–30 age limit; minimum stay five nights; cultural center and library. Must show proof of student status; no advance reservations accepted. Office open Monday–Saturday 9:30 A.M.– 6 P.M., Sunday 10 A.M.–noon.

Centre International de Paris (BVJ)
Paris Louvre, 20, rue Jean-Jacques Rousseau (1st)
Telephone: 42-36-88-18
Métro: Louvre

Paris Opéra, 11, rue Thérèse (1st)
Telephone: 42-60-77-23
Métro: Pyramides

Paris les Halles, 5, rue du Pélican (1st)
Telephone: 40-26-92-45
Métro: Palais Royal

Paris Quartier Latin, 44, rue des Bernadins (5th)
Telephone: 43-29-34-80
Métro: Maubert-Mutualité

Priority given to groups; no individual reservations and no families; showers and breakfast included. Lunch or dinner or half pension (breakfast and lunch or dinner), but the only restaurant for the four foyers is in the Paris Louvre.

Centre International de Sejour de Paris (CISP)
Kellerman, 17, boulevard Kellerman (13th)
Telephone: 45-80-70-76
Métro: Porte de Vincennes

Ravel 6, avenue Maurice-Ravel (12th)
Telephone: 43-43-19-01
Métro: Porte d'Italie
   Large, lots of extras, caters to groups, located on fringes. Ravel has access to a pool. Both open 6:30 A.M.–1:30 A.M. Showers and breakfast included; lunch or dinner served, but extra; no advance reservations except for groups. Kellerman open to ages 5–77.

Cité Universitaire (Foundation Nationale de la Cité Universitaire)
15, boulevard Jourdan (14th)
Telephone: 45-89-68-53
Métro: Cité-Universitaire
   The Cité Universitaire is a vast maze of 40 international student residences located on the edge of the city next to the Parc Montsouris (15 minutes by Métro to St-Michel). Both advance and short-notice reservations are possible, depending on residence. Foreign students and teachers are accepted from July 1 to September 30. Minimum stay is 7 to 15 days, depending on residence. There are more than 4,500 rooms, so getting something isn't impossible. Open Monday–Friday 8 A.M.–noon, 4–7 P.M.

Foyer International d'Accueil de Paris
30, rue Cabanis (14th)
Telephone: 45-89-89-15
Métro: Glacière (across from Ste-Anne Hospital)
   One of the best; good for families; rooms for disabled. Showers and breakfast included; lunch and dinner extra. Advance reservations accepted up to one month before arrival. Open Monday–Friday 8 A.M.–2 P.M.

Foyer Jacques de Rufz de Lavison: Maison d'Étudiants
18, rue Jean-Jacques Rousseau (1st)

Telephone: 45-08-02-10
Métro: Palais-Royal or Les Halles
   Accepts groups in single or double rooms; well located in center of Paris; showers and breakfast included; open July–September 7 A.M.–7 P.M.

Union Chretienne de Jeunes Filles
22, rue Naples (8th)
Telephone: 45-22-23-49
Métro: Europe or Villiers
   French YWCA; accepts women; minimum three-month stays during school year, three-day minimum otherwise. Must pay a membership fee and a processing fee. Rooms are good. Open 8:30 A.M.–midnight. Showers and breakfast included; dinner available. Accepts telephone reservations in summer.

Y & H Hostel
80, rue Mouffetard (5th)
Telephone: 45-35-09-53
Métro: Monge
   Called the Young and Happy Hostel because it is friendly and everyone has so much fun here. Perfectly located, with loads of inexpensive restaurants nearby. Reception open daily from 8–11 A.M. and 5 P.M.–1 A.M. Showers included; no breakfast served. Can reserve with a one-night deposit or arrive when they open. There is no age limit.

BIG SPLURGES

The following hotels fall into the Big Splurge category. They are higher priced and included here because their location, amenities, ambience, service, and overall appeal will suit those travelers with more demanding tastes and flexible budgets.

Shopping: Cheap Chic

Paris is wrenchingly beautiful, and so are many of its people. If you use your eyes and take in everything, you can learn more about true style in a weekend then in a lifetime's perusal of fashion magazines....

— Lucia Van der Post

Paris is a shopper's dream come true. Even those who dislike shopping at home are bound to be attracted by the unending selection of shops in Paris. The haute couture, open *marchés*, extravagant toy shops, and the magnificent displays of eye-popping jewelry, cosmetics, perfumes, antiques, and collectibles that once belonged to kings—the list goes on and on. It would take another book to properly discuss all the shopping wonders awaiting you. To get you started, I have listed major department stores, chain stores, open-air markets, *passages*, *galeries*, and finally a list of shops selling designer clothing at tremendous discount. Generally speaking, shop hours are Monday through Saturday from 9:30 A.M. to 7 P.M. Some of the smaller shops close for lunch, and everything is closed on Sunday and holidays.

VAT: VALUE-ADDED TAX, OR *DÉTAXE*

If you buy between 1,500 and 1,600F worth of merchandise in *one store*, you are entitled to a 13 to 23 percent tax refund if you are a foreigner. This refund is known as a *détaxe*. The paperwork is simple, filled out by you and the store. You will need to have your passport available for identification. On the *détaxe* form, you will be asked to state whether you want the refund mailed to you in a French-franc check (not recommended because it is hard to deal with in the United States and getting it takes almost forever), or to have it credited to one of your credit cards. This last option is the best, not only because it is much faster than waiting for a check to arrive, but because your credit card company will credit the refund to you in U.S. dollars on your account. It is painless and wonderful. At your point of exit from France, a customs official will stamp your documents, which you then will mail back to the store, and that is all there is to it. Generally, you must *ask* about this *détaxe*, because most smaller shopkeepers will not volunteer the information. In the large department stores there are special offices that take care of this paperwork. Yes, it does take some extra time and effort, but the savings can be significant, so persevere and insist on getting it.

SIZE CONVERSION CHART

FRENCH AND AMERICAN CLOTHING SIZES

Women's dresses, knitwear, and blouses

F	36	38	40	42	44	46	48
US	8	10	12	14	16	18	20

Women's stockings

F	1	2	3	4	5
US	8½	9	9½	10	10½

Women's shoes

F	36½	37	37½	38	39	40	41
US	5	5½	6	6½	7½	8	8½

Men's shoes

F	39	40	41	42	43	44	45
US	6	7	7½	8½	9	10	11

Men's suits

F	36	38	40	42	44	46	48
US	35	36	37	38	39	40	42

Men's shirts

F	36	37	38	39	40	41	42
US	14	14½	15	15½	16	16½	17

PREMIER PARIS SHOPPING AREAS
(Cost not necessarily an object)
AVENUE GEORGE V, AVENUE MARCEAU, AVENUE MONTAIGNE, FAUBOURG ST-HONORÉ, AND RUE FRANÇOIS 1er (1ST AND 8TH)

For window shopping and dreaming, these five premier shopping streets are to designer fashion and haute couture as the Louvre is to art. The boutiques and shops are simply not to be missed, even if you only stroll by the elegant window displays.

LE FORUM DES HALLES (1ST)

The ultramodern, multilevel complex on the site of the old Les Halles market attracts over 40 million visitors a year. In this covered wonderland there are more than 200 shops displaying the latest kicky fashions, scores of inexpensive restaurants and fast-food stalls, and walk-in hair salons offering sculpted cuts or dye jobs in glowing green or blue. The largest Métro station in the world lies under it all. It is fun to be part of the strolling crowds, if only for the experience of people-watching: you will see every kind of fashion victim imaginable.

PLACE DES VICTOIRES (1ST)
A wonderful shopping experience nestled behind Palais-Royal. After going around the circle, branch out down the side streets. This is an area of many fashion innovators and well worth serious time just to see what you will be wearing two years from now. The prices are not in the bargain department, unless you happen to hit a sale.

ST-GERMAIN-DES-PRÉS (6TH AND 7TH)
Sensational shopping can be found on the Rue de Sèvres, Rue Bonaparte, Rue de Four, Rue St-Sulpice, Rue Jacob, and the Rue de Seine, to mention only a few of the streets that line this *quartier*, which is literally packed with fashion boutiques, antiques shops, art galleries, and book shops. In fact, if you have only a short time to devote to shopping and browsing, this is where you should go.

CHAMPS-ÉLYSÉES (8TH)
While the Champs-Élysées used to be the finest address a retailer could have, today there are waves of tourists flowing up one side and down the other. Movie theaters, airline offices, banks, car dealers, and mini-malls charging top francs for everything line each side of the famous avenue. Pickpockets work both sides of the street and are pros at what they do—watch out! Reserve your time on the Champs-Élysées for sipping an afternoon drink at Fouquet's and for people-watching. Do your shopping elsewhere.

RUE DE PASSY AND AVENUE VICTOR-HUGO (16TH)
Walking down either of these shop-lined streets in the 16th arrondissement will give you an idea of what it is like to be in the upper middle class and live in Paris. You will see very few tourists, no razor haircuts, and certainly no hawkers selling T-shirts or plastic replicas of the Eiffel Tower. There are several nice sidewalk cafés if someone in your party would rather have a beer and watch the world go by.

CHAIN STORES

Inno Passy
53 rue de Passy (16th)
Métro: Passy

Hours: Mon–Sat 10 A.M.–7 P.M.

Credit Cards: MC, V

An upscale kissing cousin to Monoprix and Prisunic. This location is the best in the chain.

Monoprix
Boulevard Haussman between Au Printemps and Galeries
Lafayette (9th)
Métro: Havre-Caumartin
Hours: Mon–Sat 9:30 A.M.–6:30 P.M.
Credit Cards: MC, V

The place to buy Bourjois cosmetics (prototypes for Chanel at a fraction of the Chanel price). Also good underwear for women, children.

Prisunic
20, rue de Passy (16th)
Métro: Passy
Hours: Mon–Sat 10 A.M.–7 P.M.
Credit Cards: MC, V

A notch better than Monoprix, and one of the best in the chain.

Prisunic
52, avenue des Champs-Élysées (8th)
Métro: Franklin-D.-Roosevelt
Hours: 9:45 A.M.–midnight
Credit Cards: V

If the shopping urge strikes late in the evening, Prisunic on the Champs-Élysées will come to the rescue. This link in the chain serves an impressive 9,000 tourists and locals each day. (Because of the inadequate ratio of *caisses* [cash registers] to shoppers, you may feel as if you are in line behind all 9,000.)

DEPARTMENT STORES (*LES GRANDS MAGASINS*)

Au Printemps
64, boulevard Haussmann (9th)
Métro: Havre-Caumartin
Hours: Mon–Sat 10 A.M.–7 P.M.
Credit Cards: AE, MC, V

Billed as "The Most Parisian Department Store." Famous designer boutiques, a separate men's store, and an excellent leather department on the first floor.

Bazar de l'Hôtel de Ville (BHV)
52, rue de Rivoli (4th)
Métro: Hôtel de Ville
Hours: Mon, Tues, Thurs, Sat 9 A.M.–6:30 P.M.; Wed 9 A.M.–10 P.M.
Credit Cards: AE, MC, V
A shopping experience no do-it-yourselfer should miss. Vast kitchen, hardware, and automotive departments.

Bon Marché
38, rue de Sèvres and rue du Bac (7th)
Métro: Sèvres-Babylone
Hours: Mon–Sat 9:30 A.M.–6:30 P.M.
Credit Cards: AE, MC, V
A showplace department store with Gustave Eiffel–designed balustrades and balconies. Combines the elegant and practical. Excellent grocery department.

Galeries Lafayette
40, boulevard Haussmann (9th)
Métro: Havre-Caumartin
Hours: Mon–Sat 9:30 A.M.–6:30 P.M.
Credit Cards: AE, MC, V
Top names in fashion and many services for the tourist including an easy way to handle the VAT (*détaxe*). Gourmets and gourmands alike will want to check out the recently opened fine-foods shop, Lafayette Gourmet. This grocery store borders on the inspirational with its dazzling array of delicacies, featuring everything a gastronome could possibly want. Even dedicated noncooks will want to see this beautiful addition.

La Samaritaine
19, rue de la Monnaie (1st)
Métro: Pont Neuf
Hours: Mon, Thurs, Sat 9:30 A.M.–7:00 P.M.; Tues and Fri 9:30 A.M.–8:30 P.M.; Wed 9:30 A.M.–10 P.M.
Credit Cards: AE, MC, V
Don't miss the panoramic view of Paris from the top floor. A good place to buy Parisian-style work clothes as worn by waiters, chefs, butchers, etc.

Marks & Spencer
35, boulevard Haussmann (9th)
Métro: Havre-Caumartin
Hours: Mon–Sat 10 A.M.–6:30 P.M.

Credit Cards: AE, MC, V

Parisian branch of the London favorite. A good selection of basics. The silk lingerie is very well priced.

Franck et Fils
80, avenue Paul Doumer (16th)
Métro: Muette
Hours: Mon–Sat 10 A.M.–7 P.M.
Credit Cards: MC, V

A small, elegant department store catering primarily to the women of Paris's most expensive *quartier*. Super sales in January and July.

Tati Department Stores
4–30, boulevard Rochechouart (18th)
Métro: Anvers
Hours: Mon–Sat 10 A.M.–6 P.M.
Credit Cards: None; cash only

If you love swap meets, garage sales and basement fire sales, then Tati is for you. The crowds are legion, especially on Saturdays, but for truly amazing bargains hidden among some real junk, join the ethnic mix at a Tati. Prices defy competition, but be sure to check each item carefully because quality control is not a high priority where this much volume is concerned. *Warning*: Watch out for pickpockets!

Tati Department Stores
140, rue de Rennes (6th)
Métro: Montparnasse, St-Placide
Hours: Mon–Sat 10 A.M.–6 P.M.
Credit Cards: None

Tati Department Stores
13, place de la République (3rd)
Métro: République
Hours: Mon–Sat 10 A.M.–6 P.M.
Credit Cards: None

FLEA MARKETS (LES MARCHÉS AUX PUCES)

What to do on a Saturday or Sunday morning? Go to the flea market, of course. Wear old clothes, comfortable shoes, beware of pickpockets, and have a great time, even if you end up not buying a thing. The days of finding a fabulous antique for a few *centimes* are long gone, but you will probably find a nice keepsake or two. If you have nothing special on your list, you can just people-watch; the wildlife at the *puces* beats that at the zoo.

Aligre Flea Market
Place d'Aligre (12th)
Métro: Ledru-Rollin
Hours: Tues–Sun open until 1 P.M.
Small daily food and flea market, good for little objects, antique buttons, bric-a-brac, and cheap clothes.

Montreuil Flea Market
Porte de Montreuil (20th)
Métro: Porte de Montreuil
Hours: Sat–Mon 9 A.M.–6 P.M.
The huge market begins once you get through the long line of vendors hawking cheap trash on the bridge.

St-Ouen/Clignancourt Flea Market
Avenue Michelet at Rue des Rossiers (18th)
Métro: Porte de Clignancourt
Hours: Sat–Mon dawn until 7 P.M.
This is the most famous flea market in France, bigger than Portobello Market in London. Once you get past the piles of jeans and the East Indians selling cheap beads, head for the Marché Brion on the corner of Rue des Rossiers. It has the most expensive stalls, but also the most serious, with the best items. The Paul Bert Market, 16, rue Paul Bert, has an unusual collection of Art Deco pieces and nice antiques from the late 1890s. The entire market covers acres, so plan accordingly.

Vanves Flea Market
Avenue Georges Lafenestre (14th)
Métro: Porte-de-Vanves
Hours: Sat and Sun 9 A.M.–7 P.M.
If you like to bargain, walk along the Avenue Marc-Sangnier. The locals come here because it is a more manageable market than the big one at Clignancourt.

PASSAGES AND GALERIES

These glass-roofed arcades were built in the first part of the 19th century and were the forerunners of indoor shopping malls. Tucked off major commercial streets, mainly in the second and ninth arrondissements, they are easy to miss if you are not looking for them. It is fun to stroll through one or two if only to see a sampling of the old-fashioned shops still selling handmade dolls, fancy pipes, 78-rpm records, old books and prints, model trains, and wondrous toys. Several of the *passages* have restaurants (see *Cheap Eats in Paris*).

Galerie Colbert
6, rue des Petits-Champs (2nd)
Métro: Bourse
Next to the Bibliothèque Nationale and restored to all its 19th-century glory.

Galerie Vivienne
4, rue des Petits-Champs (2nd)
Métro: Bourse
The most beautiful arcade of all, with some of the best shops.

Passage de Choiseul
36, rue des Petits-Champs (2nd)
Métro: Bourse
Toy specialists, shoe shops, designer clothing, and more.

Passage Jouffroy
12, boulevard Montmartre (9th)
Métro: Montmartre
Musée Grévin (a wax museum), Oriental imports, used books, country-style gift shops, antique toys, marionnettes, and puppets.

Passage des Panoramas
11, boulevard Montmartre (9th)
Métro: Montmartre
The oldest *passage* of all, opened in 1800. A nice selection of engravings and a *brocante* (second-hand) shop selling antiques and gifts.

Passage Verdeau
31 bis, rue du Faubourg-Montmartre (9th)
Métro: Montmartre
Small shops featuring collectibles: old books, cameras, early rock-and-roll records, classic comics, pop posters, etc.

SHOPPING STREETS AND
OUTDOOR ROVING MARKETS

For a close look at a vital part of daily Parisian life, visit a colorful shopping street or roving food market. When you go, take your camera and watch out for pickpockets. It is guaranteed that after a walk through one of these areas, your hometown supermarket won't ever seem the same to you. Fruits and vegetables of every variety are arranged with the skill and precision usually reserved for fine jewelry store windows. Equal care and attention is given to the display of meat, fish, cheese, and fresh flowers. A few of my favorites are listed below. To locate the one closest to your hotel, ask at the desk.

SHOPPING STREETS
Rue de Buci (6th), Métro St-Germain-des-Prés
Rue Cler (7th), Métro École Militaire
Rue Lepic (18th), Métro Abbesses
Rue Mouffetard (5th), Métro Monge

OUTDOOR ROVING MARKETS
Dupleix (15th), Métro: Dupleix or La Morte-Picquet-Grenelle, open Wed and Sun
Cours la Reine (16th), Métro: Alma-Marceau or Iéna, open Wed and Sat

MARCHÉ BIOLOGIQUE (ORGANIC PRODUCE AND PRODUCTS)
Boulevard Raspail between Rue de Rennes and Rue de Cherche-Midi (6th), Métro Rennes; open Sunday morning
A fascinating organic market selling only natural and organic produce and products from wine and soap to edibles and dried herbs. Well worth a stop if you are into natural foods.

CHEAP CHIC: DISCOUNT SHOPPING

There has always been something very stylish about the French. Just the addition of the word *French* to everyday objects such as toast, jeans, silk, and even bread lifts them above the ordinary. After you have been in Paris for a day or so, you will realize that the French do not get dressed, they get turned out. You will no doubt wonder how even a modest shop girl manages to look so elegant, considering the high price tags on most items of clothing, especially the designer numbers. The answer is simple: They *never* pay full price.

Paris is heaven for finding something *très á la mode* at a fraction of retail cost, but the trick is knowing where and when to go. This section devoted to Cheap Chic is intended to help you dress like the French and, in most cases, pay much less than you would at home for the same item on sale. Remember, with discount shopping the selection will vary from day to day and from season to season. Not all shops take credit cards, so be prepared with some extra French francs. The comfort of the customer is not always a top priority. As a result, many places do not have proper dressing rooms, most are jammed with merchandise, there is limited individual attention, and, in some cases, only fragmented English is spoken. But, never mind—dedicated shoppers will press on because you are all there for the same reason: to get a bargain, and you will.

SALES (*SOLDES*)

During most of the year, when you venture into one of the designer shops, they are quiet enough for you to hear the rustle of the money being spent by Japanese customers. However, we less affluent mortals also have a chance. For the first three weeks in January and part of June and July, Paris is *on sale*. The crowds of shoppers move with dizzying swiftness, all zeroing in on the considerable savings. If you can brave these shopping pros, this is the time to go to the designer boutiques and salons and pick up a little number for about one-third of the U.S. retail price. In October, Hèrmes has its once-yearly sale. The line to get in begins the night before, with people eager to pay 50 percent less for the famous signature scarves, ties, and conservative line of clothing. Again, if you don't mind standing in line and fighting crowds packed in ten deep, then this sale is a must for you Hèrmes fans.

MONOPRIX AND PRISUNIC

Paris shopping veterans know that the Prisunic and Monoprix chains are some of the best low-cost shopping stores for good cosmetics, little cotton nightgowns, great underwear, and the last word in funky jewelry and hair ornaments. True, you probably won't want to consider their ready-to-wear department as the final word for your spring wardrobe, but you *will* want to consider them for Chanel prototype cosmetics sold at a mere fraction of U.S. prices. Both stores market these Chanel-made products under their own line, *Bourjois*. There are Monoprix and Prisunic stores throughout Paris, but two to keep in mind are Prisunic on the Champs-Élysées and Monoprix between Au Printemps and Galeries Lafayette on Boulevard Haussmann (see "Chains," page 165).

As a dedicated shopper with a black belt in the art, I know that bargain shopping can be both exhausting and frustrating until you find that fabulous Yves St-Laurent suit in your size and favorite color for 50 percent off. This type of discount shopping in Paris takes a good eye, limitless patience, and comfortable shoes. In Paris, of all places, it should also be more than a quest to track down the cheapest item available; it should be fun. Armed with Cheap Chic and a good map, you will have a great time, save money, and go home with clothes your friends will die over. *Bonne chance!*

CHEAP CHIC SHOPPING TIPS

1. Know the prices at home so you will be able to spot a bargain when you see it.

2. If you want it, can get it home, and can afford it, you should buy it when you see it. If you wait until later, it probably won't be there when you get back, or you will see it when you get home for twice the price.

3. Nothing is returnable, so be sure when you buy the item that it fits and doesn't have flaws.

4. Pack an empty, soft folding suitcase in your luggage so you can transport home all your treasures without the extra hassle and expense of mailing.

5. Take the time to do all the paperwork for the *détaxe*, and remember to turn it into the customs officials at the airport *before* you relinquish your luggage or go through customs or passport control (see *détaxe*, page 163).

6. If you are shopping at one of the *marchés au puces*, be sure to bargain. The asking price is not the price you are expected to pay. You should be able to bargain the price down by around 15 to 20 percent.

7. *Never* change money at a shop. The rate will not be in your favor. Go instead to a bank or use plastic money.

8. You can bring back $400 worth of duty-free goods acquired abroad. This is per person, per family. After the $400 point, there will be a 10 percent charge on the next $1,000, and more as the amount increases. If you ship things back home, any package worth *less* than $50 is considered an unsolicited gift and can be sent duty free. If your package exceeds $50, duty will be charged.

DISCOUNT SHOPPING AREAS

Look for signs in the windows reading *Soldes* (sales), *Dégriffés* (labels cut out), *Depot Vente* (resale), or *Rétro* (period clothing from the fifties and sixties).

RUE D'ALESIA (14TH)
Métro: Alesia
Credit Cards: Varies with each shop
Shops on both sides of the street, some with names you have heard of, others that you never will. Overstocks and last season's merchandise at good prices. The best line of attack is to go up one side and down the other to get an overview, then come back to those that seem promising. Some of the better shops are:
Evolutif, 72, rue d'Alesia
Dorothee Bis, 74, rue d'Alesia
Stock & Stock II, 92–94, rue d'Alesia
Stock System, 110–112, rue d'Alesia
Kookai, 111, rue d'Alesia
Cacharel, 114, rue d'Alesia
Daniel Hechter, 116–118, rue d'Alesia
Salles des Ventes du Particulier, 117–123, rue d'Alesia
Philippe Salvert, 122, rue d'Alesia
Alesia Discounts, 139, rue d'Alesia

RUE MESLAY (3RD)
Métro: République
Credit Cards: Varies with each shop
Fine Italian footwear at positively unbeatable prices. Discount shoe shops line the street. The best advice is to browse first, then go back and do serious buying. Finding the perfect pair of shoes takes time and patience, so don't try to squeeze this in: allow plenty of time and leave the kids and male companions at the hotel.

RUE DE PARADIS (10TH)
Métro: Château-d'Eau
Credit Cards: Varies with each shop
The best area in Paris for china and crystal, in shop after magnificent shop. Be sure to see Baccarat at 30 bis, rue de Paradis; open Mon–Fri 9 A.M.–6 P.M., Sat 10 A.M.–noon and 2–5 P.M.

RUE ST-DOMINIQUE (7TH)
Métro: Latour-Maubourg

Credit Cards: Varies with each shop

From Avenue Bosquet to Boulevard de Latour Maubourg. Clothing for men, women, and children, from designer *dégriffés* to bins of last season's T-shirts.

RUE ST-PLACIDE (6TH)
Métro: Sèvres-Babylone
Credit Cards: Varies with each shop

A magnet for serious discount shophounds. Start at Bon Marché Department Store and work both sides of the street. This is hard work if the crowds are out in force, especially at lunchtime when the office girls surge through. However, if you are willing to hang in there, you will probably find something. Best buys are in casual sportswear and teenage fashions of the moment. There are a limited number of top designers—but everything is *au courant.*

SHOPS SELLING DESIGNER CLOTHING AT A DISCOUNT

André Courrèges
7, rue de Turbigo (1st)
Telephone: 42-33-03-57
Métro: Étienne-Marcel, Les Halles
Hours: Mon–Sat 10:15 A.M.–6 P.M.
Credit Cards: None
Good selection of last season's clothes that did not sell.

Tiziano
30, place du Marche St-Honoré (1st)
Telephone: 42-60-08-98
Métro: Tuileries, Pyramides
Hours: Mon noon–7 P.M., Tues–Fri 10 A.M.–7 P.M., Sat 10. A.M.–12:30 P.M. and 2–7 P.M.
Credit Cards: AE, MC, V
Last year's collection of beautiful Italian shoes for men and women, at 30 percent off and more. Factory leftovers from Gucci, Céline, and Valentino with the Tiziano label. Wonderful!

Gianni d'Arno pour Rève de Soie
17, rue St-Marc (2nd)
Telephone: 42-36-98-73
Métro: Richelieu-Drouot

Hours: Mon–Sat 10 A.M.–6:30 P.M.
Credit Cards: None
The best-priced silk blouses in Paris in a rainbow of colors and styles. The second location on Rue Cler accepts credit cards, but has a more limited stock.

Gianni d'Arno pour Rêve de Soie
2, rue Cler (7th)
Telephone: 45-51-96-38
Métro: École Militaire
Hours: Mon–Sat 10 A.M.–noon and 3–7 P.M.
Credit Cards: V

Halle Bys
60, rue de Richelieu (2nd)
Telephone: 42-96-65-92
Métro: Bourse
Hours: Mon–Sat 10 A.M.–7 P.M.
Credit Cards: V
Clothes for men, women, and children from boots to underwear. The selection varies greatly: good one time and just so-so the next. The best choices are usually upstairs. Not on the A list, but for discount diggers, worth a pass-by.

Mendès-YSL
65, rue Montmartre (2nd)
Telephone: 45-08-52-62, 42-36-83-32
Métro: Sentier
Hours: Mon–Fri 9:30 A.M.–1 P.M. and 2 P.M.–5:30 P.M., Sat 9:30 A.M.–4:30 P.M.
Credit Cards: V
Overstocks on two levels of Yves St-Laurent Rive Gauche line and a smattering of other designer labels from the last season. If you hit it right, it's a gold mine. In December and June they have a sale and take 20 to 30 percent more off the already reduced prices.

Sodiclub
57, rue Ste-Anne (2nd)
Métro: 4-Septembre
Hours: Mon–Sat 10 A.M.–6 P.M.
Credit Cards: V
Thirty percent off on items not sold over the last year at airport boutiques. The selection varies, but quality is always tops.

Dépôt de Grandes Marques
15, rue de la Banque (take elevator to third floor)(2nd)
Telephone: 42-96-99-04
Métro: Bourse
Hours: Mon–Sat 10 A.M.–7 P.M.
Credit Cards: MC, V
An enormous selection of designer men's wear at close to wholesale. Same-year collection of suits, jackets, pants, shirts, rain gear, ties, belts. One week for alterations.

Marché du Carreau du Temple
Entire block around Eugène Spuller (3rd)
Métro: Temple
Hours: Tues–Sat 9 A.M.–6 P.M., Sun 9 A.M.–1 P.M.
Credit Cards: Depends on individual seller
If you are interested in leather or suede, this is worth a look. There are dozens of sellers hawking leather wearing apparel. Browse through to get a feel for what is available, then bargain like crazy if you find something you want.

Anna Lowe
35, avenue Matignon (8th)
Telephone: 43-59-96-61
Métro: Miromesnil, St-Philippe de Roule
Hours: Mon–Sat 10:30 A.M.–7 P.M.
Credit Cards: AE, DC, MC, V
All the top name designers, including Chanel, at reduced prices. All labels are left in; a fabulous selection of evening wear. Sensational July and mid-December sales. Fast alterations.

Bab's
29, avenue Marceau (8th)
Telephone: 47-20-84-74
Métro: Alma
Hours: Mon–Sat 9:15 A.M.–7 P.M.
Credit Cards: AE, DC, MC, V
One of the best women's discount shops in Paris. Not the *haute, haute,* but quality clothing accessories. Good dressing rooms and a helpful staff.

Bab's
89 bis, avenue des Ternes (17th)
Telephone: 45-74-02-74

Métro: Ternes
Hours: Mon–Sat 9:15 A.M.–7 P.M.
Credit Cards: AE, DC, MC, V

Cachemire First
9, rue Richepance (8th)
Telephone: 42-60-12-78
Métro: Madeleine, Concorde
Hours: Mon–Sat 9:30 A.M.–7 P.M.
Credit Cards: AE, DC, MC, V
Cashmere sweaters for men and women in more than 25 colors. Traditional styles. Also alligator handbags, wallets, and belts; suede and leather jackets. Sales in February, July, and August.

David Shiff (Club des 10)
4, rue Marbeuf (first floor; press buzzer to right of door) (8th)
Telephone: 47-20-34-25
Métro: Alma
Hours: Mon–Sat 10 A.M.–6 P.M.
Credit Cards: MC, V
A wonderful selection of quality men's clothing. They will give *détaxe* for a total purchase of 1,200F or more.

David Schiff (Club des 10)
13, rue Royale (8th)
Telephone: 42-66-43-61
Métro: Concorde
Hours: Mon–Sat 10 A.M.–6 P.M.
Credit Cards: MC, V
Not cheap, but extremely good value. Lovely women's fashions, good dressing rooms, intact labels.

Solde Trois
3, rue de Vienne (8th)
Telephone: Boutique for men, 42-94-99-67
Telephone: Boutique for women, 42-94-93-34
Métro: Europe
Hours: Mon–Fri 10:30 A.M.–6 P.M., Sat 10:30 A.M.–2 P.M.
Credit Cards: V
Well worth a safari to the edge of things to check out the wonderful selection of Lavin clothing for men and women that has not sold in the very high-priced boutique on Rue St-Honoré.

Miss "Griffe's"
19, rue de Penthièvre (8th)
Telephone: 42-65-10-00
Métro: Miromesnil
Hours: Mon–Fri 11 A.M.–6:30 P.M., Sat 3–7 P.M.
Credit Cards: AE, DC, MC, V
A good selection from new-collection prototypes or leftover stock. All the top names, including Chanel and Valentino. The nice owner, Madame Vincent, is very helpful. Free alterations ready in one or two days.

Suemaco
13, rue de Trévise (9th)
Telephone: 48-24-89-00
Métro: Montmartre
Hours: Mon–Sat 10 A.M.–6 P.M.
Credit Cards: MC, V
An excellent selection of designer men's fashion at below retail.

Eugénie Boiserie
32, rue Vignon (9th)
Telephone: 47-42-43-71
Métro: Madeleine
Hours: Tues–Sat 10 A.M.–noon and 1–6 P.M.
Credit Cards: No; cash only
Inch your way through the cluttered gift shop to the back, where Eugenie Boisérie has been providing haute couture for hire for over 30 years. Shown by appointment only, dresses and formal wear rent from 800 to 1,000F, plus a deposit.

Jean-Louis Scherrer Stock
29, avenue Ledru-Rollin (12th)
Telephone: 46-28-39-72
Métro: Gare de Lyon
Hours: Mon, Tues, Thurs–Sat 10 A.M.–6 P.M.; closed Wed
Credit Cards: None; cash only
Two rooms of haute couture by Scherrer and others at about half the original prices.

Mi-Prix
27, boulevard Victor, corner rue Desnouettes (15th)
Telephone: 48-28-42-48
Métro: Balard

Hours: Tues–Sat 9:30 A.M.–6 P.M.

Credit Cards: None; cash only

Up to 50 percent off on Maud Frizon, Walter Steiger, and Xavier David shoes. Fabulous boots in every style and color. Even though they carry some big-name clothes designers, your reason for being here will definitely be the huge collection of shoes. A great selection in size 36 (U.S. size 4½ or 5).

Catherine Baril

14–16, rue de la Tour and 25, rue de la Tour (16th)

Telephone: 45-20-95-21 (at 14–16, rue de la Tour); 45-27-11-46 (at 25, rue de la Tour)

Métro: Passy

Hours: Mon 2–7 p.m., Tues–Sat 10 A.M.–7 P.M.

Credit Cards: V

At the 14–16, rue de la Tour shop, the used clothing and accessories include all the couture stars and are in apple-pie condition. At the 25, rue de la Tour shop, the clothing is new, but is all last season's models. All the biggies are here, from Chanel to YSL. A nice staff, fair prices, a super selection, and well-lighted dressing rooms in both locations. This has the highest recommendation from savvy French shoppers.

L'Affair d'Un Soir

147, rue de la Pompe (16th)

Telephone: 47-27-37-50

Métro: Victor-Hugo

Hours: Mon 2–7 P.M., Tues–Sat 10:30 A.M.–1 P.M. and 2–7 P.M.

Credit Cards: MC, V

Silk dresses, ball gowns, hats, and elegant gloves are available here for all *soirée* goers. Sophie de Mestier and Jane du Payrat design two original collections each year for rent or sale. Many customers rent an outfit and can't bear to part with it, so they end up buying it. Expect to pay from 550F to rent and from 1,850F to purchase.

Réciproque

89, 93, 95, 97, 101, 123, rue de la Pompe (16th)

Telephone: 47-04-82-24, 47-04-30-28

Métro: Pompe

Hours: Tues–Sat 10:15 A.M.–6:45 P.M.; closed 1 week in July and all of August

Credit Cards: MC, V

The Rolls-Royce of "previously owned" designer duds for a fraction of retail. Consignments of everything from gifts and antiques to estate jewelry, shoes, bags, clothes, furs, men's wear, and more. Allow plenty of looking time. The staff is helpful.

MISCELLANEOUS CHEAP CHIC SHOPS

Jewelry

Bijoux Burma
72, rue du Faubourg St-Honoré (1st)
Telephone: 42-65-44-90
Métro: Concorde
Hours: Mon–Sat 10:30 A.M.–7 P.M.
Credit Cards: AE, DC, MC, V
The best faux jewelry in Paris at prices most anyone can afford. Of the many Bijoux Burmas in Paris, this is the best.

Perfumes and Cosmetics

Catherine Perfumes and Cosmetics
6, rue de Castiglione (1st)
Telephone: 42-60-81-49
Métro: Tuileries
Hours: Mon–Sat 9:30 A.M.–7 P.M.
Credit Cards: AE, DC, MC, V; will accept personal U.S. checks
An excellent selection of perfumes, cosmetics, scarves, and ties. They will give a tax-free price of 40 percent off if you purchase 1,500F or more worth of goods and 20 percent off if you purchase less. Mail orders to the United States have the same discounts.

Freddy
10, rue Auber (through the courtyard, up two flights of stairs) (9th)
Telephone: 47-42-63-41
Métro: Opéra
Hours: Mon–Fri 9 A.M.–6 P.M.
Credit Cards: V
Forty percent off perfumes and cosmetics if you spend at least 1,600F. If you spend less, you will still get 25 percent off.

Michel Swiss
16, rue de la Paix (second floor, via elevator) (2nd)
Telephone: 42-61-61-11
Métro: Opéra
Hours: Mon–Sat 9 A.M.–6:30 P.M.

Credit Cards: Not if you want the discount

A mob scene of international shoppers buying perfumes, scarves, women's handbags, and cosmetics. If you spend 1,600F or more, there's a 25 percent discount given, plus an additional tax discount for non-EC residents that amounts to 18 to 28 percent, depending on the product.

Sephora
66, rue Chausée d'Antin (9th)
Telephone: 42-82-06-22
Métro: Chausée d'Antin
Hours: Mon–Sat 10 A.M.–7 P.M.
Credit Cards: V

An absolutely mind-boggling collection of cosmetics, perfumes, and miscellaneous accessories. They carry all the lines, including Bourjois. No *détaxe*, but the prices are *very* competitive. Well worth a look.

Sephora
50, rue de Passy (16th)
Métro: Passy
Hours: Mon–Sat 10 A.M.–7 P.M.
Credit Cards: V

Sephora
Forum des Halles (1st)
Métro: Les Halles
Hours: Mon–Sat 10 A.M.–7 P.M.
Credit Cards: V

Souvenirs

Destination Paris
9, rue du 29-Juillet (1st)
Telephone: 49-27-98-90
Métro: Tuileries
Hours: Mon–Sat 10:30 A.M.–7:30 P.M.
Credit Cards: AE, MC, V

Skip the trashy tourist souvenirs on Rue de Rivoli and shop here for imaginative and whimsical memorabilia to celebrate your trip to the City of Light. Loads of clever items under 60F.

Limoges boxes, gifts

La Dame Blanche
186, rue de Rivoli (1st)

Telephone: 42-60-67-12
Métro: Palais-Royal
Hours: Mon–Sat 10 A.M.–6:30 P.M.
Credit Cards: AE, DC, MC, V

The windows are jam-packed with boxes, gloves, silk scarves and ties, Haviland china, hand-painted plates, etc. Don't let this confusing clutter deter you from one of the best selections of hand-painted Limoges boxes in Paris. Michael, the owner, speaks English and offers a 15 percent discount if you spend 1,200F or more.

Used Books

Tea & Tattered Pages
24, rue Mayet (6th)
Telephone: 40-65-94-35
Métro: Falguière
Hours: Mon–Sat 10 A.M.–7 P.M.
Credit Cards: No; cash only

Vivacious American expatriate in Paris Kirsti Chavane opened her used-book store a year ago and it has been an unqualified hit ever since. The average price for a good used paperback (in English) is 25F and only 40F for a hardback non-fiction. She also stocks gifts, loads of fantasy teapots, and cards. Stop by for an hour or so and have a cup of tea and a muffin from the San Francisco Muffin Company (see *Cheap Eats in Paris*, page 97), or a slice of illegally rich fudge or a walnut brownie. Kristi is friendly and plugged into the Paris scene, and I guarantee you won't regret a visit to her two-level shop.

Sweaters

Pierre Vivez
6, rue des Saussaies (8th)
Telephone: 42-65-26-54
Métro: Champs-Élysées Clemenceau
Hours: Mon–Sat 10 A.M.–7 P.M.
Credit Cards: MC, V

A large collection of traditional pure wool sweaters for men and women. Also cotton T-shirts, jackets, and skirts for summer. Everything is guaranteed washable.

Watches

Capion
9, rue Auber (9th)
Métro: Opéra

Hours: 9:30 A.M.–7 P.M.
Credit Cards: AE, MC, V
Watches for every person on your list, at prices starting at 45F.

Unusual Gifts

Baïkal
15, East Lacharrière (11th)
Telephone: 48-06-00-37
Métro: St-Maur
Hours: Mon–Sat 10 A.M.–8 P.M.
Credit Cards: AE, MC, V
For wonderful one-of-a-kind gifts for friends and yourself, *do not miss* Michael Monlaü's lovely shop. Michael loves Americans, speaks perfect English, and is only too willing to spend lots of time with you to help you find just the right gift. The prices are within all budgets.

READERS' COMMENTS

While every effort has been taken to provide accurate information in this guide, the publisher and author cannot be held responsible for changes in any of the listings due to rate increases, inflation, dollar fluctuation, the passage of time, or management changes.

Cheap Sleeps in Paris is updated and revised on a regular basis. If you find a change before I do, or make an important discovery you want to pass along to me, please send a note stating the name and address of the hotel or shop, the date of your visit, and a description of your findings. Your comments are very important and I follow through on every letter received. Thank you.

Send your comments to Sandra A. Gustafson (Cheap Sleeps in Paris), c/o Chronicle Books, 275 Fifth Street, San Francisco, CA 94103.

INDEX OF HOTELS

INDEX OF OTHER OPTIONS

Other travel guides by Sandra A. Gustafson:
Cheap Eats in Paris
Cheap Eats in London
Cheap Sleeps in London

Available in Spring 1993:
Cheap Eats in Italy
Cheap Sleeps in Italy

Available at your local bookstore. For a color catalog of all our books, call or write:

Chronicle Books
275 Fifth Street
San Francisco, CA 94103
1-800-722-6657